Christian Truths Necessary for Salvation

by Nicholas Byfield
with chapters by C. Matthew McMahon

Copyright Information

Christian Truths Necessary for Salvation by Nicholas Byfield, with chapters by C. Matthew McMahon
Edited by Therese B. McMahon
Transcribed by Blake Gentry for Republication

Published by Puritan Publications
A Ministry of A Puritan's Mind®
Crossville, TN
www.apuritansmind.com
www.puritanpublications.com

This Print Edition, 2019
Electronic Edition, 2019
Manufactured in the United States of America

ISBN: 978-1-62663-685-9
eISBN: 978-1-62663-344-5

Table of Contents

Meet Nicholas Byfield
by C. Matthew McMahon Ph.D., Th.D.

Not many Christians today are familiar with Nicholas Byfield (1579–1622). This is a tragedy since his writings are akin to that sweetness of Thomas Watson with the practicality of Jeremiah Burroughs. Byfield was a Calvinistic puritan divine, a native of Warwickshire, the son of Richard Byfield. Nicholas entered Exeter College, Oxford, in 1596, at "aged 17 at least," which gives 1579 as the latest date for his birth. On his portrait there is an inscription, "Anno Dei 1620 Aetatis suae 40," making 1579 the earliest date. The second inscription on his portrait shows that he was born in the last third of the year.

He spent four years at the university, but because he was an unruly student, he did not graduate. Not long after, he was converted, and took his first position exercising his ministry in Ireland. On his way there he preached at Chester, and was prevailed on to remain as one of the city preachers. He lectured at St. Peter's church, and became extremely popular.

In 1611 he entered into a controversy on the question of the Sabbath in a curious way. John Brerewood, one of his catechists, had been trained by Byfield in strict Sabbatarian habits. Consequently, when the boy went to London to serve as an apprentice, he refused to do his master's errands on

Sundays, such as fetching wine and feeding a horse, and obeyed only under compulsion. The lad wrote to Byfield with his case of conscience, and was told to *disobey*. His uncle, Edward Brerewood, first professor of astronomy in Gresham College, noticed the boy's depression, and, learning its cause, gave him contrary advice, taking the ground that the fourth commandment was laid only on masters. Brerewood opened a correspondence with Byfield on the subject. The discussion was not published until after both Brerewood and Byfield were dead. It appeared as, "A Learned Treatise of the Sabaoth..." and it was published in 1630. Byfield's part in it is curt and harsh; his writing and disposition bothered Mr. Breerwood, who charges his correspondent with "ignorant fantasies." However, proof of fantasy is only servant to the truth of Scripture.

Later, Byfield was admitted to a position of ministry at Isleworth. There he was diligent in preaching twice every Sunday, and in giving expository lectures every Wednesday and Friday. He kept up his public work until five weeks before his death. He suffered from stones for fifteen years, and this may very well have been the catalyst of his death. He died on Sunday, September 8, 1622.

His portrait, has on it, "Mr. Nicholas Byfield, minister some times in the City of Chester, but last of Isleworth, in the county of Midellsex, where he deceased on the Lord's Day September the 8th, *anno domini* 1622, aged nearly 43 years. The next day after his death he was opened by Mr. Millins, the surgeon, who took a stone out of his bladder of this form, being of a solid substance 16 inches compass the length way, and 13 inches compass in thickness, which weighed 35 ounces in weight." This corresponds closely with the account given in William Gouge's epistle prefixed to Byfield's "Commentary upon the second chapter of the First Epistle of Saint Peter," published in 1623. William Gouge was present at the autopsy and makes the measurements of the calculus 15 inches about the edges, above 13 about the length, and almost 13 about the breadth. By his wife, Elizabeth, Byfield had at least eight children, of whom the third was Adoniram.

Byfield's works are numerous, and most of them went through many editions, some as late as 1665. They confer a Reformed and Calvinistic position and were popular Reformation documents in his day. His first publication was, "An Essay concerning the Assurance of God's Love and of Man's Salvation," published in 1614, which has been republished by Puritan Publications. This was followed by, "An Exposition upon the Epistle to the Colossians...being the substance of neare seaven yeeres weeke-dayes sermons," published in 1615. Benjamin Brook gives abridged titles of fourteen works (eight being posthumous), adding "several sermons," but these are included in one or other of the collections of his works. "The Marrow of the Oracles of God," published in 1620, was the last thing published by Byfield himself, is a collection of six treatises, which includes one separately enumerated by Brook, "The Promises; or a Treatise showing how a godly Christian may support his heart," *etc.*, 1618, 12mo, also republished by Puritan Publications.

We are working diligently to publish all of Byfield's available works and have already published a good portion of them concerning the Christian walk and a Spirit-filled life. (Those marked with an * have been or are being published by Puritan Publications.)

1. *An Essay on the Assurance of God's Love and Man's Salvation*, 1614.*
2. *An Exposition on the Epistle to the Colossians*, 1615.

3. *Directions for the private reading of the Scriptures,* 1618.*

4. *A Treatise shewing how a godly Christian may support his Heart with comfort against all the Distresses which, by reason of any Affliction or Temptation, can befall him in this Life,* 1618.*

5. *The beginning of the Doctrine of Christ, or a Catalogue of Sins,* 1609.*

6. *The Marrow of the Oracles of God,* 1620.

7. *Commentary or Sermons on the second Chap, of the 1 Epis. of St. Peter,* 1623.

8. *Sermons on the first ten verses of the third Chap, of the 1 Epis. of St. Peter,* 1626.—The two last were published, with additions, entitled, "A Commentary upon the whole First Epistle of St. Peter," 1637.

9. *An Exposition of the Apostle's Creed,* 1626.*

10. *Answer to Mr. Breerwood's Treatise of the Sabbath,* 1630.

11. *The Signs of God's Love,* 1630.*

12. *The Practice of Christianity; or, an Epitome or Mr. Rich. Rogers's Seven Treatises.*

13. *The Principal Grounds of the Christian Religion.**

14. Several Sermons.*[1]

---

[1] Part of the information about Byfield is taken in part from the *National Dictionary of Biography* UK, from Benjamin Brook's *Lives of the Puritans*, Volume 2, and from Daniel Neal's *Neal's Puritans.*

Does the Biblical Word "The" Save Anyone from Hell?

by C. Matthew McMahon, Ph.D., Th.D.

23,814 times the word "the" is used in the English Bible. This word "the" is used in innumerable passages, and is part of the Word of God. The word "a" is used 6,309 times. The word "so" is used 3,349 times. The word "it" is used 6,202 times. Now, try and take any one of these individual words and use them as the sole basis of a "Gospel" message. Let us utilize the word "the". Could the Spirit use, in and of itself, the word "the" as a means to convert the soul? Let me be more specific before you consider your answer. Let us place a man on a desert island. He is not familiar with the Bible at all and really knows nothing about Jesus Christ. One day, a small boat washes up on shore and he looks therein and finds an old skeleton holding a copy of the Scriptures. Now this copy has been soaking in the water of the ocean's waves and the rains falling on it for some time. It is a wonder that it was not lost. In excitement he grabs the book and opens it up, being so desolate on this island all alone, and with nothing but his tattered clothes he decides to read. He opens this book (which, for sake of argument, he doesn't know it is a bible because of its ruined nature), and cannot make out anything in the book except, on a few pages, he can make out the word "the." In other places he can see the word "a" and the word "so." After reading over these words, could such a man be saved by *that* "Gospel content?" No, he could not. The word "the" is *not* the Gospel. The word "so" is not the Gospel. Nor is the word "a" the Gospel. They have no meaning behind them, no message.

Now, there is a point to be made here that one should not miss in considering the book that Byfield has written. Let us not be quick to assume that the Spirit works "hap hazzardly" with any single word in the Bible. As much as the word "the" *is* Scriptural, it is not enough to save, even if we piled up all 23,000 instances of it in one pile, to convert someone. Why? There is no Gospel content or message contained within the word "the."

To believe *the Gospel,* or those Christian truths necessary for salvation, there must be content, and substance. The activity of faith after regeneration must believe ... *something.* In an unpublished sermon on Acts 26:18, Jonathan Edwards states, "Now it is certain that every sinner that becomes good there is a last moment of his being bad, and a first moment of his being good, a last moment of his being in a state of damnation and a first moment of his being in a state of salvation or that there is a time before which if he had died but one moment he would have gone to hell, and after which if he had died he would have gone to heaven, this is self-evident, or which is all one he is made immensely a better man in a moment than he was before..."[2] There was a specific moment when the person was lost, but then there is an instantaneous "transaction" to his removal from the Kingdom of Darkness into the Kingdom of God's beloved Son. He moves from "lostness" to "savedness" in a moment. That moment is called *regeneration,* where *the Word of God* is made *effectual* to him, not merely the word "it," "the," "so," or "a".

---

[2] Jonathan Edwards, Unpublished Sermon: Acts 26:18, page 1 Nov. 1747. Found in John Gerstner, *The Rational Biblical Theology of Jonathan Edwards*, Volume 3, 152.

William Ames explains the process of regeneration vividly, "As for man, receiving is either passive or Active. Phil. 3:12 says, "I apprehend because I have been apprehended." The passive receiving of Christ is the process by which a spiritual principle of grace is generated in the will of man. Eph. 2:5, "He hath quickened..." Active receiving is an elicited act of faith in which he who is called now wholly leans upon Christ as his savior and through Christ upon God. John 3:15-16, "Whoever believes in him..." 1 Peter 1:21, "Through him believing God..."[3] This is important to note that *leaning*, here, is believing and understanding. Without this "fiducia" or "faith" men cannot be saved. Is it not a wonder why so many sit under Gospel preaching for so long? They are gaining more and more information about the Gospel, in pieces, and then the Spirit, on a particular day the Gospel is presented and explained, makes that knowledge of Christ a reality in faith for them through regeneration. They believe something more than "it," "the," "so," or "a." There must be substance to the Gospel for belief in the Gospel. As Pascal said, "The substance of faith consists of Jesus Christ."[4]

Martin Lloyd Jones preached a very good sermon on the phrase "But God..." from Romans 5:8. Now, what shall we do with such a thing since it is just a bit more for our friend on the desert island to look at than the words "it," "the," "so" and "a"? People were converted as a result of Jones' sermon. Lloyd Jones only preached on "But God..." Does this change the idea of Gospel content and substance to be believed? To the contrary, you may have missed the important aspect of the statement. I

---

[3] William Ames, *The Marrow of Theology*, (Baker Books: Grand Rapids, MI, 1997), Page 159.
[4] Blaise Pascal, *The Mind on Fire*, (Multnomah Press, Portland, OR: 1989), 164.

said he "preached a sermon" on this phrase. Do you see what I am getting at? Let us assume that no one in his congregation had ever heard anything about Jesus Christ before, and it was simply by an amazing act of God's sovereign providence that they all came together to hear this man speak at this time for the very first time. Lloyd Jones then reads, "But God…" and closes his bible. Now, do you know what happened? Nothing. Nothing at all. People sat in the pew waiting to hear what would come next, knowing that "But God" is quite incomplete. No one was converted at that point in the sermon. No "evangelism" had taken place. The people *waited* for him to continue. Do you know what happened next? Well, Lloyd Jones *preached* through a *sermon* greater than an hour long on what these two little words *meant* in the context of the book of Romans, and in the context of the Gospel. Can God save a man on two words? Certainly he can, but only after they have had a thorough explanation of what they *mean;* and those two words are filled up with solid, biblical Gospel content! If after an hour and a half of preaching the content and message of the Gospel was clearly given, certainly, "But God…" can be used by the Spirit to convert *all those people* sitting and listening to the herald preaching the Word of God. I think people have a difficult time understanding that an explanation of a text must surround the reading of a text in order for preaching and conversion to take place.

Jonathan Edwards said, "a remarkable work of grace I have sometimes formerly, in reading the apostle's discourse to Cornelius, (Acts 10) wondered to see him so quickly introduce the Lord Jesus Christ into his sermon, and so entirely dwell upon him through the whole of it, observing him in this point very widely to differ from many of our modern preachers: but latterly this has not seemed strange, since Christ has appeared to be the substance of the Gospel, and the center in which the several lines of divine revelation meet. Although I am still sensible there are many things necessary to be spoken to persons under pagan darkness, in order to make way for a proper introduction of the name of Christ, and his undertaking in behalf of fallen man."[5] Dwelling on Christ is the first step to precision when explaining the Gospel. "Jesus wept" may be included in the larger presentation of the Gospel, but it, in and of itself, is *not* the Gospel. The Gospel has certain non-negotiable qualities in order to be believed. What are those non-negotiable traits?

Nicholas Byfield is going to demonstrate the necessary Christian truths of the Gospel. He will talk quite a lot about the Old Testament. The Gospel *can* be found there. He will talk quite a lot about the New Testament. The Gospel *can* be found there as well, and even in more clarity. But in either testament, the substance of the Gospel for all believers remains the same, and focuses on Jesus Christ. God has bound himself to save in a specific manner with a specific message. Men cannot be saved by general revelation of nature. Men are only saved through special revelation, which argues a specific message (otherwise such revelation would not be needed). Consider that Byfield is very liberal in using the entire Bible, all of the Word of God, to explain all those necessary truths in order to understand God's message of salvation, though not every passage in the Bible contains the Gospel. He will show that "faith" is believing and trusting in the divine object (Jesus Christ) of a specific message (the good news) and knowing that such an object of knowledge *is good.* No one would ever trust in anything they did not know to be good for them in that way, and Byfield will

---

[5] Jonathan Edwards, *Brainard's Journal.*

setup these Gospel truths in such a way that you might come to know them in a simpler manner.

From my study,
C. Matthew McMahon, Ph.D., Th.D.
October, 2019

Introduction[6]

To the most noble Lady, the Lady Dorothy, Countess of Northumberland; and to the highly honored Ladies, her daughters. To the Lady Dorothy Sydney, and the Lady Lucy Hay: Nicholas Byfield wishes the abundance of true grace and peace.

Right honorable,

I have long since undertaken (as in the course of my ministry you have often heard) to extract out of all theology contained in the Scriptures, their main principles. In other words, such doctrines which are fundamental, and absolutely necessary to be known of as many as are *to be saved.* This project ought to be well accepted of all sorts of Christians, that wish their own good; partly in respect of the necessity of the doctrines here collected under their several heads; and partly in respect of the apparent evidence of the proofs of Scripture, which are such as make an infallible demonstration to the conscience, by the express light contained in them. Also, partly because the uses which may be made of the several principles, are everywhere abundantly shown.

---

[6] The original title to this work was the following: The Pattern of Wholesome Words, or a collection of such truth as are of necessity to be believed to salvation, separated out of the body of all theology. Made evident by infallible plain proofs of Scripture. And withall, the several uses such principles should be put to, are abundantly shown. A project much desired, and of singular use for all sorts of Christians. BY NICHOLAS BYFIELD, Preacher of God's Word at Isleworth in Middlesex. "Keep the true pattern of wholesome words, which thou hast heard of me in faith and love, which is in Christ Jesus," (2 Timothy 1:13). LONDON, Imprinted by F.K. for Samuel Man, dwelling in Paul's Churchyard, at the Sign of the Swan. 1618.

And inasmuch as the Lord has been pleased to give some testimony to my endeavors in this, in public preaching, I am not out of hope, but that the printing of those principles may be profitable to many godly and plain-hearted Christians, that desire the plainest manner to understand the meaning of their heavenly Father's will.

I humbly dedicate this work to your honors, and pray your acceptation and the patronage of it. And give me leave in the view of the world to signify this way, both my observance of the many noble and excellent virtues which are eminent in each of your honors, as also my unfeigned thankfulness for the many favors I have received and for the countenance and encouragement of my ministry. I account it a singular mercy of God, that any labors of mine should find acceptation with persons of so high place and quality, or any way be successful to the prospering of any part of the work of God's grace in your hearts.

Now the God of all consolation fill your noble breasts with all riches of the true grace that is in Jesus Christ; that you may abound in the knowledge of the mysteries of his kingdom in all judgment, and love of the truth which is according to godliness, and in all those gifts which may be found to honor, and praise, and glory in the revelation of Jesus Christ.

Your Honor's in all service,
NICHOLAS BYFIELD
Isleworth, March 27, 1618.

CHAPTER 1:
Containing the Nature and Use of This Treatise

The purpose and drift of this treatise is to effect three things:

1. First, to extract out of all theology contained in the Scriptures such truths as are of *necessity* to be believed for salvation; the knowledge of this is required of everyone. In the defense of this we should be ready to suffer the most extreme things, even death itself; and which we should account the very characters of true religion, the distinct knowledge of which we should lay up, as great riches.

2. Secondly, to gather out of the Scriptures such evident proofs of each of those truths, as might make a full assurance and establishment of heart in their particular belief.

3. Thirdly, to point out the several uses we should make of these fundamental truths, and for what excellent purpose the may serve us all the days of our life.

Consider the benefit of attending to this course. Singularly great would the profit of this project be, if there were a heart in man to use a little diligence in matters of so great concern. Is it not a marvelous benefit in this contending world for a man to know distinctly what truths are infallible; and to have the truths that are absolutely necessary to be believed, separated from such as a man may be ignorant of, and yet be saved?

And for the second thing, it is certain, that most Christians know their grounds but by *hearsay*, and by the common judgment of others. Where here they may be informed of them so as to know them by proofs of Scripture, which with a little labor they may commit to memory, as seed-plots of contemplation.

And for the third, what is the reason that commonplace divinity is so out of use in popular teaching, or that catechisms are looked on so dully, and learned or taught with so little profit? The use of such doctrine has not been distinctly shown. So, as men think of principles, as of certain inferior truths, they do this because they see other points in textual course handled with directions for their use. Where it is certain that no doctrines in religion have more abundant use in the life of man, nor more urged with variety of uses in the Scriptures, than the heads or main points of a biblical catechism.[7]

And for the warrant of the project, it is evident that the apostles made a separation of truths, and extracted the fundamental truths out of the main body of doctrine, and those they delivered to churches, as the common treasure of all the saints. And they did this both for their honor and use as they are described by diverse titles.

They were called "the principles of the praises of God," (Hebrews 5:12). "The principles of the doctrine of Christ," (Hebrews 6:1). "The doctrines of foundation" in the same place. "The pattern of wholesome words," (2 Timothy 1:13). "The form of the knowledge of the truth," (Romans 2:20). "The form of doctrine, into which they were delivered," (Romans 6). All which titles show their singular use.

Now if any man may ask me how I will know a principle, I answer by these marks:

First, it is such a truth to be believed, as is contained in the express words of Scripture. So, as I take a principle to be a

---

[7] Keep in mind that Byfield lived before the 1647 Westminster Confession of Faith and Catechisms.

doctrine plainly expressed in the Word, and so differ from doctrines that are deduced from the Scriptures only by consequence, or are there but in dark and obscure words.

Secondly, principles are first truths, that is such as have been from the beginning, and have been believed in all ages of the church.

Thirdly, they are such truths as being stubbornly and willfully denied, the whole building falls down, and men do not hold the foundation. Besides, any man may be guided in this, that will make use of the judgment of the churches in their creeds and confessions, and catechisms; though it is true that if men narrowly observe most catechisms, they either have no principles, or else they have more than principles, such truths as are strong meat, and so prove to be hard sayings to the weak. Neither am I so transported with any other over-weaning of myself in this project, but that with all readiness I shall subject my endeavors in it to the correction of the learned and godly. If my labor may provoke others more sufficient to perfect this work with such exactness, as is further requisite, I shall rejoice in it, and think I have attained a happy end.

I do not doubt, but that this labor may be of great use for younger divines to point out a way, how they may catechize with more profit by making the uses of every principle, as they teach the grounds to the people. Yes, it is one part of the Sabbath day's best employment in sermons to treat in this, or the same manner; and so to let the people be truly informed concerning the characteristic truths in their religion, with their use in their conclusion.

Lastly, it will be some contentment to the ingenious minds to see the principles cast into some method for helping memory and quickening of delight, and an easier way of learning them.

CHAPTER 2:
The Method of the Principles

The principles concern either the fountain and origin of doctrine and knowledge, which is the Scripture or Word of God; or the subject of knowledge, which is God himself.

In God we consider: His nature and his works.

The works of God, as the principles take notice of them, are: creation and providence.

The providence of God must be considered either in general, or as it concerns only man. The providence of God, as it concerns man, has principles that look on him in his fourfold state:

The estate of innocence.

The estate of corruption or misery.

The estate of grace, where the principles consider:

1. The means of grace, *viz.* election in God and redemption in Christ.

2. The subject of grace, *viz.* the church.

3. The degrees, or sorts of grace: *viz.* justification, and sanctification.

-In the estate of glory, where we find:

1. Of the resurrection of the dead.

2. Of the last judgment.

3. Of the glory of heaven.

CHAPTER 3:
Of the Scriptures

"For the whole Scripture is given by inspiration of God," (2 Timothy 3:16).

The origin or fountain of knowledge is the Scripture, that is, the books of the Old and New Testament, and those books were first called *Scripture*, in the New Testament.

There are two principles concerning Scripture:

1. That they are the very word of God, or they flow from God by divine inspiration.

2. That they are perfect, without defect or error, every way sufficient of themselves alone, to guide us in all things needful to salvation, without adding anything to them, or diminishing anything from them.

For the first, that they are by divine inspiration, is infallibly evident from the testimony of the Scriptures themselves, such as these, (2 Timothy 3:16 before recited):

"So that ye first know this, that no prophecy of the Scriptures is of any private interpretation. For the prophecy came not in old time by the will of man: but holy men of God spake as they were moved by the Holy Ghost," (2 Peter 1:20-21).

And for our more abundant satisfaction, there are other testimonies that prove the Scriptures to be the very word of God, and these both external and internal.

The external testimonies are such as these:

1. The divine revelations, with which they were graced from heaven. For God was visibly present with Moses, the writer of the law, and God testified his presence also by the

cloud and smoke about the ark, in the tabernacle, and temple. Fire from heaven devoured the sacrifices, and God gave answers by the Urim and Thummim.

2. The fulfilling of the prophecies uttered in the Scriptures in several ages.

3. The testimony of the church in all ages, acknowledging the books of Scripture, as the pure Word of God.

4. The final confession of the martyrs, who at their death justified so much, and willingly died in the defense of the truths contained in the Scriptures.

5. The conversion of the souls of men by the power of the Scriptures, and the comfort the godly find in them in all afflictions.

6. The miraculous calling of the men, as we may see in Moses and the Apostles, that wrote the Scriptures.

The internal testimony is the witness of God's Spirit, who in the hearts of the godly avouches so much, and this is a testimony proper to the household of God. So much for the first principle.

The second principle is, that the Scriptures are perfect, which these places show:

"That the man of God may be absolute, being made perfect unto all good works," (2 Timothy 3:17).

"The law of the Lord is perfect, converting the soul, the testimony of the Lord is sure, and giveth wisdom unto the simple," (Psalm 17:7).

"But though that we, or an angel from heaven preach unto you otherwise, than that which we have preached unto you, let him be accursed," (Galatians 1:8).

"Therefore whatsoever I command you, take heed you do it: thou shalt put nothing thereto, nor take ought therefrom," (Deuteronomy 12:32).

"For my mouth shall speak the truth, and my lips abhor wickedness. All the words of my mouth are righteous, and there is no lewdness, nor frowardness in them," (Proverbs 8:7-8).

First, for instruction: the consideration of which principles may serve us for diverse uses; both for instruction and reproof, for trial and for consolation:

1. First, we should here be persuaded to study the Scriptures with all diligence, and to strive to get the plenteous knowledge of them. Searching those divine words, and exercising ourselves in the morning and evening; accounting so much to be added to our riches, as we get of this excellent knowledge.

"Search the Scriptures: for in them you think to have eternal life, and they are they, which testify of me," (John 5:39).

"Let the Word of God, or Christ dwell in you plenteously in all wisdom, teaching and admonishing your own selves," (Colossians 3:16).

"But his delight is in the law of the Lord, and in his law doth he meditate day and night," (Psalm 1:2).

Laboring by all means to acquaint our children, and family with them.

"And thou shalt rehearse them continually unto thy children, and shalt talk of them, when thou tariest in thy house, and as thou walkest by the way, and when thou liest down, and when thou risest up," (Deuteronomy 6:7).

2. Since they are of God, and so perfect, we should rest on the directions, and comforts we find in them, and establish our hearts in all things we learn out of them, "For whatsoever

things are written aforetime, are written for our learning, that we through patience, and comfort of the Scriptures, might have hope," (Romans 15:4). They are a sure word; we may rest upon them, (2 Peter 1:20) as believing that every word of God is pure, and that God will make them good to such as trust in them, (Proverbs 30:5-6).

3. We should care to read and hear these Scriptures with all due preparation and attention, and high estimation, receiving them as the Word of God, and not of man: (1 Thessalonians 2:13) laboring to bring clean hearts, and a meek and teachable spirit to them, as being able to save our souls, (James 1:21-22) with a resolution to do whatever God requires in them.

4. We should love them above all treasures, accounting them dearer than thousands of gold and silver, and reckoning the sentences learned out of Scriptures, as the fairest ornament which can adorn us, (Deuteronomy 11:18-19, Psalm 119:72).

5. We should therefore make them the rule of all our actions, and come continually to them to see whether our works are worked in God, and showing the power of the Word in the demonstration of its apparent life, in commanding all our particular actions, that men may see the light of the word in the light of our good works. "That we may be blameless and pure, and the sons of God, without rebuke in the midst of a naughty and crooked nation, amongst whom you shine as lights in the world," (Philippians 2:15). "And as many as walk according to this rule, peace shall be upon them, and mercy upon the Israel of God," (Galatians 6:16). "Thy word is a lamp unto my feet, and a light unto my path," (Psalm 119:105).

Yes, we should try and search daily the secrets of our hearts by it, as that which only can do it. "For the Word of God is lively, and mighty in operation, and sharper than any two-edged sword, and entereth through even unto the dividing asunder of the soul and the spirit, and of the joints and the marrow, and is a discerner of the thoughts and intents of the heart," (Hebrews 4:12).

6. We should therefore in all questions and controversies let the Scriptures judge, and "think of no man, above what is written," (Galatians 1:7, 1 Corinthians 4:6, Isaiah 8:20). So much for instruction.

Secondly, these principles reprove the papists and carnal Protestants, and the godly too. The papists are here reproved:

1. For making the authority of the Scriptures to depend upon the testimony of the church, where the church is built upon the Scriptures, "And are built upon the foundation of the Apostles and Prophets; Jesus Christ himself being the chief cornerstone," (Ephesians 2:20).

2. For not holding it to be sufficient without traditions, contrary to the express word, "That the man of God may be absolute, being made perfect unto all good works," (2 Timothy 3:17).

3. For withholding the Scriptures from the common people, keeping from them the sight of their Father's will, contrary to the word, "Search the Scriptures: for in them you think to have eternal life, and they are they which testify of me," (John 5:39). "Let the word of God dwell in you plenteously in all wisdom," (Colossians 3:16).

4. For judging controversies without them, contrary to the commandment, "To the law, and to the testimony. If they speak not according to this word, it is because there is no light in them," (Isaiah 8:20).

The carnal Protestants are here reproved:

1. For their miserable neglect of the reading, hearing, meditation, and the care to yield obedience to the Scriptures: yes, for the wretched neglect of the very buying of the Bible for their use, and the use of their families, and for daring to live without the preaching of the word in times of spiritual famine.

2. For their vile, audaciousness, that dare live in such sins, as they hear threatened in the Scriptures, profanely despising the warning daily given them, (Isaiah 30:11-12, Jeremiah 23:9-10).

3. For their scorning and deriding of such, as honor the Word, and frequent its hearing. "But draw near hither, ye sons of the sorceress, the seed of the adulterer and the whore. Against whom do ye sport yourselves? against whom make ye a wide mouth, and draw out the tongue? are ye not children of transgression, a seed of falsehood," (Isa. 57:3-4).

4. For their irreverence, when they come to the house of God to hear, (Ecclesiastes 5:1).

Yes, even the godly themselves ought to be humbled by the consideration of all this:

1. For their distractions in the hearing and reading of the Word.

2. For neglecting the counsels and directions given out of the Word.

3. For not resting on it through unbelief.

4. For too much aptness to receive opinions, if they come from men they account godly, though they have no warrant from the Word. There are traditions on the right hand, as well as on the left. So much for reproof.

Thirdly, we may all try ourselves, what we are by our respect of the Scriptures. If we love and hear the Word, we are of God, "He that is of God, heareth God's Word: ye therefore hear them not, because ye are not of God," (John 8:47). God's people are a people in whose hearts is God's law, (Isaiah 51:7, Psalm 37:31).

Lastly, it may be a singular consolation to all such as find the Word of God to testify with them. It does not matter what the world says or thinks of us; if we can find that the Word of the Lord is good concerning us, our hearts may be at rest. When God speaks peace by his Word, and we may be sure we are in the right way, when we follow the directions of the Word.

CHAPTER 4:
Of God

Here are the principles concerning the fountain of knowledge: the subject of knowledge is God, who must be considered in two ways: first, in his nature; secondly, in his works.

Concerning God considered in his nature, there are four principles:

1. That he is, that is, that there is a God.
2. That he is glorious in nature.
3. That he is three in Persons.
4. That he is one in essence.

1. For the first, that there is a God, is everywhere apparent in every leaf, yes almost in every line of Scripture; and therefore, I spare quotations, it being beyond the reaches of doubt, that the Scripture says so.

And against all seeds of atheism, men may keep in their minds these other testimonies; both inward and outward.

The inward testimonies that prove there is a God, are these:

1. The horror of conscience that befalls men after the committing sin, dreading a supreme Judge; which terrors we see are oftentimes such as no outward thing can still.

2. The testimony of the Holy Spirit infallibly satisfying the godly in this.

3. The revelation of God to the hearts of his people, daily finding him in the use of his ordinances, which presence of God they likewise miss if they sin presumptuously.

The external testimonies are taken from the works of God; either more generally in the world; or more specifically in the church. The world testifies that there is a God:

1. In respect of the creation of it: this huge frame could not make itself, and therefore of necessity there must be some being that gave it being.

2. By the motion that is in it. For that shows there is a supreme mover.

3. By the strange judgments that fall on the wicked, sometimes in the very act of sinning, and sometimes at the very instant of the wishes of the wicked persons.

4. In that all nations have at all times acknowledged a God.

In the church God has proved himself to be:

1. By apparitions: God has shown himself by certain forms, or signs of his presence: thus Adam, Noah, Abraham, Isaac, Jacob, and Moses "saw God."

2. By the miracles worked beyond all the course of nature, as when he raised dead men, divided the sea, made the sun go backwards. So we see the proof of the first principle.

2. That God is also marvelously glorious in his nature, these places show: Psalm 29 all through it.

"Again, he said, I beseech thee shew me thy glory. And he answered," (Exodus 33:18).

"And one cried to another, and said, Holy, holy, holy is the Lord of hosts: the whole world is full of his glory," (Isaiah 6:2-3).

"Who only hath immortality, and dwelleth in the light that none can attain unto, whom never man saw, neither can see, unto whom be honor, and power everlasting, Amen," (1 Timothy 6:16).

And how can he be but exceedingly glorious, when as he *is:*

1. Incorporeal, beyond the perfection of bodily things, "God is a Spirit," (John 4:24).

2. Eternal without any beginning, "Before the mountains were made, and before thou hadst formed the earth, and the world, even from everlasting to everlasting thou art our God," (Psalm 90:2).

3. Infinitely immense, and incomprehensible. "Is it true indeed that God will dwell on the earth? Behold the heavens, and the heavens of heavens are not able to contain thee, how much more unable is this house that I have built," (1 Kings 8:27). "Do not I fill heaven and earth, saith the Lord," (Jeremiah 23:24).

4. Immutable without shadow of change, "Every good gift, and every perfect gift is from above, and cometh down from the Father of lights, with whom is no variableness, neither shadow by turning," (James 1:17). "God is not as man, that he should lie, neither as the son of man, that he should repent: Hath he said, and shall he not do it? And hath he spoken, and shall he not accomplish it?" (Numbers 23:19).

5. Omnipotent, so as nothing is impossible to him, "But our God is in heaven, he doth whatsoever he will," (Psalm 115:3). "And Jesus beheld them, and said unto them, with men this is impossible, but with God all things are possible," (Matthew 19:26). "I know that thou canst do all things, and that there is no thought hidden from thee," (Job 42:2).

6. Omniscient, so as he knows all things universally, and perfectly, "Great is our Lord, and great is his power, his wisdom is infinite," (Psalm 147:5). "O the depth of the riches both of the wisdom and knowledge of God! How unsearchable are his judgments, and his ways past finding out?" (Romans 11:33).

"Neither is there any creature, which is not manifest in his sight: but all things are naked and open unto his eyes, with whom we have to do," (Hebrews 4:13).

7. Most holy: without sin in himself, and hating sin in others. "For thou art not a God that lovest wickedness: neither shall evil dwell with thee," (Psalm 5:4). "And one cried to another, and said, Holy, holy, holy is the Lord of hosts," (Isaiah 6:3).

8. All-sufficient and independent. "The Lord appeared to Abraham, and said unto him: I am a God all-sufficient, walk before me, and be thou upright," (Genesis 17:1). "And God answered Moses: I am that I am," (Exodus 3:14). "For of him, and through him, and for him are all things: to him be glory forever. Amen," (Romans 11:36).

9. Most merciful, "So the Lord passed before his face, and cried: The Lord, the Lord, strong, merciful, and gracious. Reserving mercy for thousands, forgiving iniquity, and transgression, and sin, and not making the wicked innocent," (Exodus 34:6-7). Consider all of Psalm 136.

10. Lastly, immortal, so as he can never die or cease to be. "Now unto the King everlasting, immortal, invisible, unto God only wise, be honor and glory forever and ever. Amen," (1 Timothy 1:17).

1. And all this should teach us:

1. To adore and fear this great and glorious God. "O the deepness of the riches both of the wisdom and knowledge of God," (Romans 11:33,35-36).

2. To dilate our hearts in a special manner in his praises. There is never such a subject of praise as God is. His praises should take up all people, by all means, and at all times, while we have any being. "Blessed be the Lord God, and blessed be his glorious name forever, and let the whole earth be filled with his

glory. Amen, amen," (Psalm 72:18-19). "O sing unto the Lord all the earth, bless his name, declare his glory from day to day; the Lord is great and greatly to be praised: give unto the Lord the glory due unto his name," (Psalm 96:1). "Praise ye the Lord; for praise is comely," (Psalm 147:1). Also, the whole of Psalm 148, and Revelation 5:9.

3. With special admiration to set our hearts and affections upon him, to love him with all our souls, and all our might. "And the Lord thy God will circumcise thine heart, and the heart of thy seed, that thou mayest love the Lord thy God with all thine heart, and with all thy soul, that thou mayest live," (Deuteronomy 30:6).

O these beauties should make us wonderfully in love with God! who is only worthy to be accounted of a good nature. "And he said unto him, Why callest thou me good? there is none good, but one, even God," (Matthew 19:17).

4. With all diligence to seek all good at his hands.

5. With all thankfulness to acknowledge what good we receive from him; yes acknowledging all we have to be from him, "Every good gift, and every perfect gift is from above, and cometh down from the Father of lights," (James 1:17). What are we, that so great a God should set his heart upon us to show us mercy?

6. Seeing he is a Spirit, and so transcendently glorious, and knows all things, we should resolve to serve him with all possible affection, putting on the beauties of the best holiness we can get, when we come into his presence, "God is a Spirit, and they that worship him must worship him in Spirit and truth," (John 4:24).

7. Let us forever hate sin, and strive for all possible imitation of his holiness. "Extend thy loving kindness to them that know thee, and thy righteousness unto them that are

upright of heart," (Psalm 36:10). "But as he which hath called you is holy, so be you holy in all manner of conversation. Because it is written: Be you holy, for I am holy," (1 Peter 1:15-16). "We know that whosoever is born of God sinneth not: but he that is begotten of God, keepeth himself, and the wicked toucheth him not," (1 John 5:18-19). "Therefore I abhor myself, and repent in dust and ashes," (Job 42:6).

8. Finally, we should strive to get an increase in the true knowledge of our glorious God, we should study his glory; but then we must be warned, when we go about this study, to look to diverse things.

1. We must repent of our sins, for this knowledge requires a clean heart.

2. We must bring a humble and teachable mind, "Them that are meek will he guide in judgment, and teach the humble his way," (Psalm 25:9).

3. Let the Word be your guide. Look for him in the Word. You must captivate your reason, and advance your faith.

4. You must go to the Son to reveal the Father. Pray to Christ to show you the Father, "No man hath seen God at any time: the only begotten Son, which is in the bosom of the Father; he hath declared him," (John 1:18).

5. Pray for the Spirit of revelation to form this in you, and resolve to get your heart established in the knowledge of God, by many prayers.

6. Observe him in his *image* in his children, get affection to them, and live much with them. "He that loveth not, knoweth not God; for God is love. No man hath seen God at any time; if we love one another, God dwelleth in us, and his love is perfect in us," (1 John 4:8,12,16). So much for instruction.

2. Here is also a great matter of humiliation for those vile atheistic thoughts, and base conceits which are in men's

minds concerning God; and for the daily neglect of God's presence, forgetting him days without number, and for daring to sin in his sight; but especially for a lack of those burning desires after God, and that surpassing love of his glorious nature.

3. Thirdly, here is singular consolation to all those that are assured they are in favor with God. Why do our hearts not say, "We have none in heaven but God? and do desire none in earth with him?" (Psalm 73:23), seeing he is so all-sufficient, able to do us so much good, and our plentiful reward, (Genesis 17:1) and knows our ways, (Psalm 1:6) and entertains his people with so much grace, (Psalm 36:7-8) and the rather because he will never change, and loves you with an eternal love, (James 1:17, 2 Timothy 2:13, Numbers 23:19).

This should be the life of our lives, it is eternal life by no other means to know him to be ours in Christ, (John 17:3, Jeremiah 9:24). So much of the second principle.

3. The third principle is, that there are three Persons in the Trinity, which may be proved two ways:

1. That there is more than one person: "Furthermore God said, Let us make man in our own Image, according to our likeness," (Genesis 1:26).

2. That there are three in number, "And lo the heavens were opened unto him, and John saw the Spirit of God descending like a dove, and lighting upon him. And lo a voice came from heaven, saying; This is my beloved Son, in whom I am well pleased," (Matthew 3:16-17). "Go therefore and teach all nations, baptizing them in the name of the Father, and the Son, and the Holy Ghost," (Matthew 28:19). "The grace of our Lord Jesus Christ, and the love of God, and the communion of the Holy Ghost be with you all. Amen," (2 Corinthians 13:13). "And I will pray the Father, and he shall give you another

Comforter, that he may abide with you forever," (John 14:16-17,28). "But when the Comforter shall come, whom I will send unto you from the Father," (John 15:26). "For there are three which bear record in heaven; the Father, the Word, and the Holy Ghost: and these three are one," (1 John 5:7). These three were called in the Old Testament, *the Lord, the Angel of the Lord*, and *the Spirit of God*: and in the New, *the Father, the Son,* and *the Holy Spirit.*

The use should be:

1. To teach us to conceive of God with all possible adoration of his glorious condition, who has in the manner of his nature what is beyond the reach of men or angels: you must believe that this is so, though reason cannot tell you how it is; let it suffice you to know that it is. You shall know more how it is, both when your knowledge is grown on earth, and when you come to your perfect age in heaven.

2. When you come to worship God, make conscience of it, that you do not rob any of the Persons of their glory: But know that there are three Persons, not just one Person.

3. Learn from the Word and works of God in your course of life, to give each Person his glory, as it is written of him, or done by him.

4. This may be an unspeakable comfort to you, if you consider what the blessed Trinity is to you. Your holiness and happiness was conceived, decreed, framed, purchased, renewed, and shall be forever testified by three in heaven, "For there are three which bear record," (1 John 5:7). Genesis 1:26 as stated before. So much for the third principle.

4. That there is but one God, is proved in these places, "Hear, O Israel, the Lord our God is Lord only," (Deuteronomy 6:4).

"Thus saith the Lord, the King of Israel, and his Redeemer, the Lord of hosts: I am the first, and I am the last, and without me is there no God. Fear ye not, neither be afraid: have not I told thee from that time, and have declared it? ye are even my witnesses. Is there a God beside me? yea, there is no God; I know not any," (Isaiah 44:6, 8).

"Hear O Israel, the Lord our God is one Lord," (Mark 12:29).

"We know that an idol is nothing in the world, and that there is none other God, but one," (Ephesians 4:5-6, 1 Corinthians 8:4).

The uses are these:

1. Adore him, whom all creatures are bound to serve and acknowledge, who has no partners in his supreme sovereignty. "All nations, whom thou hast made shall come and worship before thee O Lord, and shall glorify thy name: For thou art great, and dost wondrous things, thou art God alone," (Psalm 86:9-10).

2. Love him alone, or above all. He knows those that love him, and show it by serving him only, "The Lord our God is Lord only: And thou shalt love the Lord thy God with all thine heart, and with all thy soul, and with all thy might," (Deuteronomy 6:4-5). Mark 12:29-30 as stated before.

3. It should cause us to repent, that we ever relied on anything other than him, learning hereafter forever to rely on him in our most desperate extremities, as these places show, (Deuteronomy 32:37-39, Isaiah 37:16, 1 Samuel 2:2-3).

4. We should therefore keep the unity of the Spirit in the bond of peace, as is urged, (Ephesians 4:3,6).

5. We should therefore use but one Mediator to him, "For there is one God, and one Mediator between God and man: Which is the Man Christ Jesus," (1 Timothy 2:5).

6. Lastly, how happy are his people? They are most sure to prosper and grow, as from the consideration of this principle is shown, (Isaiah 44:6-8 with coherence). Here we find the nature of God. The works of God follow. His works are either of creation or providence.

CHAPTER 5:
Of the Creation

"Thou art worthy, O Lord, to receive glory, and honor, and power: for thou hast created all things, and for thy will's sake they are, and have been created," (Revelation 4:11).

There are five principles concerning *creation:*

1. That the world had a beginning, and was not eternal, "In the beginning God created the heaven and the earth," (Genesis 1:1). "When there were no depths was I begotten; when there were no fountains abounding with water," (Proverbs 8:24). "As he hath chosen us in him before the foundation of the world," (Ephesians 1:4).

2. That this world and all things in it was made by God, "God that made the world, and all things that are therein," (Acts 17:24). "All things were made by it, and without it was made nothing, that was made," (John 1:3). "By the word of the Lord were the heavens made, and all the host of them by the breath of his mouth," (Genesis 1:1, Psalm 33:6). "Knowest thou not, or hast thou not heard, that the everlasting God, the Lord hath created the ends of the earth," (Isaiah 40:28). "For by him were all things created, which are in heaven, and which are in earth: things visible, and invisible," (Colossians 1:16).

3. That all was made of nothing. "Before God, whom he believed: who quickeneth the dead, and calleth those things which be not, as though they were," (Romans 4:17). "Through faith we understand, that the world was ordained by the word of God, so that the things which we see are not made of things which did appear," (Hebrews 11:3).

4. That God made all things only by his word. He spoke it, and it was created. He said, let it be, and it was so, (Genesis 1:1, Hebrews 11:3, Psalm 33:6,9 all recited before).

5. That all things in their creation were made good, "And God saw that all that he had made, and lo it was very good," (Genesis 1:31, 2:1).

The use may be:

1. For information. The glory of the Lord shall endure forever. He shall rejoice in his works, (Psalm 104:31).

2. For instruction, and so the Scripture teaches us by the creation the following points:

1. To fear him, and stand in awe of him, even all the inhabitants of the earth, who are the work of his hands, (Psalm 33:6-8).

2. To study the knowledge of these works of his; to remember them, contemplate of them, and praise his workmanship, and admire his glory, that does "great things, and unsearchable, yea marvelous things without number," (Job 9:10-11). Shall we not "sing unto the Lord all our life, and praise our God while we live," (Psalm 104:33), seeing, "The heavens declare the glory of God, and the firmament sheweth the work of his hands," (Psalm 19:1) and "the invisible things of him, that is, his eternal power and Godhead are seen by the creation of the world, being considered in his works," (Romans 1:20). Let us remember that God gave a Sabbath, which has a purpose for us to remember the glory of God in creation.

3. To observe the distinct glory of every person, admire that Son, by whom God made the worlds, (Hebrews 1:3, Colossians 1:16) and that the Spirit, sitting on that first chaos of void and darkness, first hatched it, (Genesis 1:2).

4. To acknowledge God's sovereignty, let him take whom he will away, who can say, "what doest thou?" "God will

not withdraw his anger, and the most mighty helps stoop under him," (Job 9:13).

5. Upon all occasions, and in all distresses to seek to him for help, assistance and succor, (Psalm 124:8, 134:3). Yes, we should be believing in him, though we see no hope in respect of outward means, (Romans 4:17, Hebrews 11:3, Isaiah 37:16).

And as this is true of affliction, and outward distresses; so is it true of all spiritual distresses about the means or matter of holiness. For God himself uses the word *create* in both, to show us that it is lawful for that reason to rest upon him, "I create the fruit of the lips to be peace," (Isaiah 57:19). "Create in me a clean heart," (Psalm 51:10), so it is also applied to good works, (Ephesians 1:10) and to our protection in general, (Isaiah 4:4-5). To show that if it was as difficult to make heaven and earth at first out of nothing, yet God will do it, and has power to do it.

6. To teach us compassion to all creatures, we should love the work of his hands, and not be cruel to them, or void of pity.

These principles may also serve for reproof of wicked men:

1. For not fearing God, and not trembling before him, as "Fear ye not me, saith the Lord? Will ye not be afraid at my presence, which have placed the sand for the bounds of the sea, by a perpetual decree, that it cannot pass it," (Jeremiah 5:22-23).

2. For not regarding his works, "And the harp, and viol, and timbrel, and pipe, and wine are in their feasts: but they regard not the work of the Lord, neither consider the work of his hands," (Isaiah 1:12).

3. For hardening themselves in their sins, notwithstanding God's threatenings, (Job 4:13, 15-16, 21).

4. And lastly, for consolation to all that put their trust in him, (Psalm 119:5-6).

He can dispose of all, since the earth is the Lord's, and all that is in it. O, what is man that God should be mindful of him, and give him such preeminence over the works of his hands? (Psalm 8:5-8, Proverbs 8:31). So much of creation.

CHAPTER 6:
Of God's Providence

"For of him, and through him, and for him, are all things. To him be glory forever. Amen," (Romans 11:36).

The principles concerning God's providence are:

1. That God knows, and takes continual notice of all things, "The eyes of the Lord in every place behold the evil, and the good," (Proverbs 15:3). "These seven are the eyes of the Lord, which go through the whole world," (Zechariah 4:10). "Neither is there any creature which is not manifest in his sight, but all things are naked and open unto his eyes, with whom we have to do," (Hebrews 4:13). "Who abaseth himself to behold things in the heaven, and in the earth," (Psalm 113:6).

2. That God upholds and governs and disposes of the world, so as all things continue through him, "They continue even to this day by thine ordinances: for all are thy servants," (Psalm 119:91). "But Jesus answered them: My Father worketh hitherto, and I work," (John 5:17). "He giveth to all life, and breath, and all things: For in him we live, and move, and have our being," (Acts 17:25,28). "He causeth grass to grow for the cattle, and herb for the use of man, that he may bring forth bread out of the earth. The lions roar after their prey, and seek their meat at God. All these wait upon thee, that thou mayest give them food in due season: Thou givest it to them, and they gather it; thou openest thy hand, and they are filled with good things. Again, if thou send forth thy Spirit, they are created, and thou renewest the face of the earth," (Psalm 104:14,21,27-28,30).

3. That the providence of God reaches to all things; even the smallest things are governed, and upheld by God. "For of

him, and through him, and for him, are all things: To him be glory forever. Amen," (Romans 11:36). "Are not two sparrows sold for a farthing, and one of them shall not fall on the ground without your Father: Yea, and all the hairs of your head are numbered," (Matthew 10:29-30). "Which covereth the heaven with clouds, and prepareth rain for the earth, and maketh the grass to grow upon the mountains. Which giveth to beasts their food, and to the young ravens that cry. He giveth snow like wool, and scattereth the hoarfrost like ashes. He casteth forth his ice like morsels, who can abide the cold thereof? He sendeth his word, and melteth them: he causeth his wind to blow, and the waters flow," (Psalm 147:8-9,16-18).

4. That of all creatures, God has most care and respect of man. "And I took my solace in the compass of his earth, and my delight is with the children of men," (Proverbs 8:31). "What is man, say I, that thou art mindful of him? And the son of man, that thou visitest him?" (Psalm 8:3-4). "For it is written in the law of Moses, Thou shalt not muzzle the mouth of an ox, that treadeth out the corn; doth God take care for oxen? Either saith he not altogether for our sakes? For our sakes no doubt it is written, that he which ploweth, should plow in hope; and he that thresheth in hope, should be partaker of his hope," (1 Corinthians 9:9-10).

5. That the good or evil which befalls man, is not without God's providence. "Or shall a trumpet be blown in a city, and the people be not afraid? Or shall there be evil in a city, and the Lord has not done it?" (Amos 3:6).

6. That he does whatsoever pleases him in heaven and in earth, "But our God is in heaven, he doth whatsoever he will," (Psalm 115:3). "For thou (O Lord) hast done as it pleased thee," (Jonah 1:14). "I know, that whatsoever God shall do, it shall be forever: to it can no man add, and from it can none diminish:

For God hath done it, that they should fear before him," (Ecclesiastes 3:14).

7. That God's dominion is everlasting, "The Lord shall reign forever, O Zion, thy God endureth from generation to generation: Praise ye the Lord," (Psalm 146:10).

The uses are:

1. For information. This is a glorious subject to meditate on, and if we search into it distinctly, there are many things admirable in God's government; such as:

1. First, the vice-regency of Christ his Son, "Who being the brightness of his glory, and the engraved form of his person, and bearing up all things by his mighty word," (Hebrews 1:3).

2. Secondly, the splendor of the means he uses, even kings on earth are his servants, "The king's heart is in the hand of the Lord, as the rivers of waters: he turneth it whithersoever it pleaseth him," (Proverbs 21:1). Yes, angels in heaven, O the admirable glory of the government of angels in the world, as is shown in a shadow in Ezekiel 1:4-15.

3. The variety of means he has, and can raise; even all the armies in heaven and earth.

4. His working sometimes without means, (Genesis 2).

5. His working against means sometimes, (Psalm 105:12-16). The sun must stand still. Fire must not burn. The sea must not drown.

6. The extent of his government; what a work to order all things?

7. The preservation of all the sorts of things even by the word of God. By succession perpetuating his creation; and supporting all things, providing daily for them.

8. The destruction he makes among the creatures, (Psalm 104:29). By deluge, fire, sword, pestilence and tumbling down monarchies, (Psalm 68:1).

9. The ordering of the disorders of the world, turning sin to good, as an apothecary does poison; and directing evil instruments, wicked men, to punish the wicked, or to correct the godly. To see how God looks one way, and they another. Nebuchadnezzar intends to satisfy his own pride, revenge, ambition, covetousness. Yet, God guides it to another use, even to correct his people, which he shows by burning his rod, (Isaiah 10:5-6, Isaiah 14:5-6,29) and God directs the evil actions of the wicked to a good end, such as the Jews in killing Christ.

10. But especially his admirable disposing of all things, notwithstanding the infinite multitude of all things in the world, which is shadowed in the wheels, (Ezekiel 1:15).

11. All this to be done without labor, or vexation: say therefore, as "My soul praise thou the Lord: O Lord my God, thou art exceeding great, thou art clothed with glory and honor. O Lord how manifold are thy works! In wisdom hast thou made them all: the earth is full of thy riches," (Psalm 104:1, 24). "Who can express the noble acts of the Lord, or show forth all his praise?" (Psalm 106:2). "Save us, O Lord our God, and gather us from among the heathen, that we may praise thy holy name, and glory in thy praise," (Psalm 106:47). "Let them therefore confess before the Lord his loving kindness, and his wonderful works before the sons of men," (Psalm 107:8). "And let them offer sacrifice of praise, and declare his works with rejoicing," (Psalm 107:22). Psalm 113:2-5, and consider the whole psalm.

2. The second use is for reproof and confutation:

1. Of such atheists, as say God does not see, or not regard, "Yet they say the Lord shall not see; neither will the God of Jacob regard it," (Psalm 94:7).

2. Of such, as acknowledge chance or fortune.

3. Of the discontentment that is in man with their condition. David calls himself a beast for this, "So foolish was I, and ignorant: I was a beast before thee," (Psalm 73:22): an excellent Psalm all the way through.

4. Of security of wicked men. If God governs, woe to them. "Whither shall they go from thy Spirit? or whither shall they fly from thy presence? If they ascend into heaven, thou art there; if they lie down in hell, thou art there," (Psalm 139:7-8). "He is wise in heart, and mighty in strength, who hath been fierce against him, and hath prospered? He removeth the mountains, and they feel not, when he overthroweth them in his wrath," (Job 9:4-5). "The righteous shall see it and rejoice; and all iniquity shall stop her mouth," (Psalm 107:42). "The Lord keepeth the strangers, he relieveth the fatherless and widow: but he overthroweth the way of the wicked," (Psalm 146:9).

3. Thirdly, the doctrine of God's providence should teach us diverse duties.

1. Take no thought of what you shall eat, you are at God's finding, "Therefore take no thought, saying, what shall we drink? or wherewith shall we be clothed?" (Matthew 6:31). Cast your care upon God, for he cares for you. "Cast all your care upon him, for he careth for you," (1 Peter 5:7). "Cast thy burden upon the Lord, and he shall nourish thee: he will not suffer the righteous to fall forever," (Psalm 55:22).

Say with Abraham, God will provide, "Let your conversation be without covetousness, and be content with those things that ye have; for he hath said, he will not fail thee, neither forsake thee," (Hebrews 13:5).

2. Be patient in adversity, and show it:

1). By restraining grief and sorrow in yourself, "I should have been dumb, and not have opened my mouth, because thou didst it," (Psalm 39:9). "So Samuel told him every whit, and hid nothing from him: Then he said, It is the Lord, let him do what seemeth him good," (1 Samuel 3:18). "My son refuse not the chastening of the Lord, neither be grieved with his correction," (Proverbs 3:11-12). Affliction does not come out of the dust.

2). By not using ill means.

3). By not fearing the rage of any creature, "And I say unto you my friends be not afraid of them that kill the body, and after that are not able to do any more," (Luke 12:4-7). "Are not two sparrows sold for a farthing? and one of them shall not fall on the ground without your Father," (Matthew 10:28-30). "Wherefore let them that suffer according to the will of God, commit their souls to him in well doing, as unto a faithful Creator," (1 Peter 4:19).

4). By seeking God, though we see no means, for he has a thousand ways that we do not know of.

3. Seek all good things at his hands, he has the disposing of all.

4. Acknowledge all good things from him, as Psalm 147, all over. Serve him in all means, and sacrifice not to your own nets, "Therefore they sacrifice unto their net, and burn incense unto their yarn, because by them their portion is fat, and their meat plenteous.

5. Do not trust in your own projects, nor in the means, "O Lord I know that the way of man is not in himself, neither is it in man to walk and to direct his steps," (Jeremiah 10:23). "Therefore he humbled thee, and made thee hungry, and fed thee with manna, which thou knewest not, neither did thy fathers know it, that he might teach thee, that man liveth not by bread only, but by every word that proceedeth out of the mouth of the Lord doth a man live," (Deuteronomy 8:3). "Except the Lord build the house, they labor in vain that build

it; except the Lord keep the city, the keeper watcheth in vain. It is in vain for you to rise early, and to lie down late, and eat the bread of sorrow; but he will surely give rest to his beloved," (Psalm 127:1-2).

But commit your way to God, and trust upon him, "And delight thyself in the Lord, and he shall give thee thy heart's desire," (Psalm 37:4).

Pray God to direct the works of your hands, "And let the beauty of the Lord our God be upon us, and direct thou the works of our hands upon us, even direct the work of our hands," (Psalm 90:17).

6. If God governs, do good and always be assured, as "And men shall say, verily there is fruit for the righteous; doubtless there is a God that judgeth in the earth," (Psalm 58:11).

7. Observe God's works, keep a catalog of experiments, "Who is wise, that he may observe these things? For they shall understand the loving kindness of the Lord," (Psalm 107:43).

And make known his deeds, talk of his wondrous works. Remember the marvelous works he has done, "Praise ye the Lord, because he is good, for his mercy endureth forever: who can express the noble acts of the Lord or show forth all his praise?" (Psalm 106:2-5).

8. Shall we not forever be afraid of him, that so mightily and daily governs? "He hath made everything beautiful in his time: also he hath set the world in their heart, yet cannot man find out the beginning even to the end. I know, that whatsoever God shall do, it shall be forever: To it can no man add, and from it can no man diminish: For God hath done it, that they should fear before him," (Ecclesiastes 3:11,14).

4. The fourth use is for consolation to the godly:

Our bones and hairs are numbered, "He keepeth all his bones, not one of them is broken," (Psalm 34:20). "Yea all the hairs of your head are numbered, fear not therefore, you are of more value than sparrows," (Luke 12:6-7).

He knows our way, "For the Lord knoweth the way of the righteous," (Psalm 1:6).

Our tears are in his bottle, "Thou hast counted my wanderings: put my tears into thy bottle, are they not in thy register?" (Psalm 56:8).

He will not leave us nor forsake us, "Let your conversation be without covetousness, and be content with those things that you have: For he hath said, I will not leave thee nor forsake thee," (Hebrews 13:5).

No good things will he withhold, "For the Lord God is the Sun and Shield unto us: the Lord will give grace and glory, and no good thing will he withhold from them that walk uprightly," (Psalm 84:11). "Can a woman forget her sucking child, that she should not have compassion on the son of her womb? yea, they may forget, yet will I not forget thee. Behold, I have graven thee upon the palms of my hands; thy walls are continually before me," (Isaiah 49:15-16).

He that believes shall not be ashamed. So much for the providence of God in general. Now we will consider man specially, which looks first on the estate of man in innocence.

CHAPTER 7:
Of Man's First Estate in Innocence

"Only lo, this have I found, that God hath made man righteous: but they have sought many inventions," (Ecclesiastes 7:31).

There are two principles concerning man's first estate.

1. God originally made man after his own image. "Furthermore God said, Let us make man in our own Image, according to our own likeness, and let them rule over the fish of the sea," (Genesis 1:26). "For a man ought not to cover his head, forasmuch as he is the Image of God," (1 Corinthians 11:7). "And they have put on the new man, which is renewed in knowledge after the image of him that created him," (Colossians 3:10).

2. Secondly, this image of God chiefly consisted in knowledge, holiness, and righteousness, "Only lo, this have I found, that God hath made man righteous: but they have sought out many inventions," (Ecclesiastes 7:29). "And put on the new man, which after God is created in righteousness, and true holiness," (Ephesians 4:24).

Note, that I say, chiefly (as that which is a principle); otherwise man was created after the image of God in the following manner:

1. First, in respect of his substance; and so man is the image, either of the,

1. Being of God, or,

2. Of the manner of his being.

1. Of his being, as he has in him a spirit, a nature:

1. Spiritual and incorporeal

2. Immortal

3. Invisible

4. Intelligible

2. Of the manner of his being: for as in man is one soul, and yet diverse faculties, as cogitation, memory, will, and so is there in God one essence, and three Persons.

2. Secondly, in respect of his eminency, excellency, and dominion above, and over all other creatures, resembling the lordship of God the Lord of all, "Furthermore God said, Let us make man in our Image, according to our likeness, and let them rule over the fish of the sea, and over the fowl of heaven, and over the beasts, and over the earth, and over everything that creepeth and moveth on the earth," (Genesis 1:26). "Thou hast made him to have dominion in the works of thine hands: thou hast put all things under his feet," (Psalm 8:6-8). For if the man is God's image for the sovereignty he has in the family, as 1 Corinthians 11:7 and the magistrate for his superiority in the commonwealth, (Psalm 82) much more man in general for dominion over all.

3. Thirdly, in respect of gifts, and so in three ways:

1. In respect of knowledge, for in the mind of man, there is hidden, a resemblance of God's wisdom to know God, his will, and works with the natures and properties of them.

2. In respect of original justice, which stood in the rectitude of his nature, the spirit subject to God, the soul to the spirit, the body to the soul without any sin.

3. In respect of freedom of will. There are four sorts of free wills:

1. Only to good; so in good angels, and the blessed.

2. Only to evil; so in devils and the wicked.

3. Partly to evil, and partly to good; so in the regenerate on earth.

4. So to good, as it might be to evil; so in Adam. The power of his freedom was such as he could do all things convenient to his estate; whether,

1. Works of nature, as eat, sleep, walk, rise, *etc.*

2. Works of policy; as govern his family, observe peace, etc.

3. Or, Works of religion:

1. Internal; to love, fear, and trust in God.

2. External; to teach, pray, and sacrifice.

The uses for all this follows:

1. We should inform ourselves of God's marvelous love to man in his creation, which appears not only in the time he made him which was the last created, when he had provided all things made for him; but in the place he had in paradise, and in the manner: both of making his body and soul. He did not say, let it be; but as it were, framed all with his own hands; the man of the dust, the woman of the rib.

And of inspiring his soul, he breathed the breath of life into him, "And the LORD God formed man of the dust of the ground, and breathed into his nostrils the breath of life; and man became a living soul," (Genesis 2:7). He gave birth to his soul as it were a divine spark or particle of God; he is therefore called the Father of spirits, (Hebrews 12:9, Zechariah 12:1, Acts 17:28).

And in both he says, "let us make," calling all the Trinity to care and workmanship. But especially that he should as it were, be made like God himself; and therefore, let us sing, as, "What is man that thou thus mindest him," (Psalm 8:3).

Of true blessedness, in which it consists, *viz.* not in idleness, riches, lust, pleasure, sports, *etc.*, for none of all this was in paradise, yet Adam lived happy and perfectly.

2. The second use is for instruction, and so it should teach us diverse duties:

1. To God; and so first we should with all thankfulness affectionately acknowledge his love to man.

2. It should instruct man earnestly to study and endeavor, to know God, to fear, to resemble him, and to praise his workmanship.

For these were the ends of man's creation, no other creatures could reach it; therefore, God made man reasonable. We do not answer the goal of our creation if we do not make God in some sort visible by our holiness, and praise his works.

2. The second duty is to ourselves, and so it should teach us:

1. First, to care for the precious and immortal soul, that God has breathed into us above all, "For what shall it profit a man, though he should win the whole world, if he lose his own soul? or what shall a man give for the recompense of his soul?" (Matt. 16:26). What should we cherish as it pertains to temporal things, when our souls are created to the possession of eternal blessedness?

2. To be patient, and trust on God in distress, "Be not far from me, because trouble is near; for there is none to help me," (Psalm 22:11).

3. To lament our fall.

4. To study our recovery, and we see here what to seek, *viz.* knowledge and goodness.

5. To long for the time mentioned, "When we shall be satisfied with his image," (Psalm 17:15).

3. The third duty is towards men:

1. First, not to wrong man: for he is God's image, "Who so sheddeth man's blood, by man shall his blood be shed: for in the image of God hath he made man," (Genesis 9:6).

2. Love one another, especially where this image is repaired: for we were created to this end, that we should delight in one another.

3. The third use is for reproof, confutation, and humiliation.

1. For our insensibleness, forgetfulness, and incapableness of these considerations, especially for our lack of lamentation for the ruins in our nature.

2. For our horrible neglect of knowledge and goodness, without which man is more like a beast; yes, in respect of sin like a devil.

3. Of the papists about pictures of God: most dishonorably they would mend God's draught by dumb pictures; yet God has here given us a picture, his image.

CHAPTER 8:
Of the Fall of Man

"Only lo, this have I found, that God hath made man righteous: but they have sought many inventions," (Ecclesiastes 7:29).

The misery of man in his estate of corruption must be considered two ways: in its cause and in its parts.

Its cause was the fall of our first parents, concerning which are these principles:

1. That our parents Adam and Eve fell, and lost speedily the happiness in which they were created, as appears in Genesis 3:7, and in this way they lost God, paradise, and God's image. And that they lost it speedily appears in that the devil is called a murderer from the beginning, and the fall is presently related after the narrative of his innocence in creation.

2. That this loss befell them only for their own grievous sin, (Genesis 3) "Wherefore as by one man sin entered into the world, and death by sin: and so death went over all men, forasmuch as all men have sinned," (Romans 5:12). Also see Ecclesiastes 7:29 as before.

3. That by their sin we are all defiled and deprived of the glory of God, Romans 5:12 as before. "Likewise then as by the offense of one, the fault came on all men to condemnation: so by the righteousness of one, the benefit abounded toward all men to the justification of life. For as by one man's disobedience many were made sinners: so by the obedience of one shall many also be made righteous," (Romans 5:18-19).

The uses follow: The uses of these woeful principles may be first for information, and so we should study to satisfy and settle our hearts more at large concerning two things.

1. The one is the grievousness of the first offense.

2. The other is the justice of God in deriving the loss to us.

1. For the first, there are many things that may assure us that the sin of our first parents was a most grievous sin: for it admits fearful aggravations; as,

1. That they dare venture all their happiness about so small an advantage to them. If we think it was a small offense to eat an apple; think with it, it was a desperate wickedness to venture eternal life for the possession of an apple.

2. This was God's first commandment that he gave them, and to neglect God so soon in a thing, in which they might so easily have obeyed, must necessarily appear to be desperate wickedness.

3. This sin was committed, when they had no inward concupiscence to tempt them, nor that proneness of nature, that is in man now to sin.

4. They offended when God had abundantly provided for them; they lacked nothing that was good for them.

5. They in this violated the whole law, because they broke the agreements which were made between God and them: according to that, "For whosoever shall keep the whole law, and yet faileth in one point, he is guilty of all," (James 1:20).

6. Because it was a sacramental fruit: to cast bread to dogs is no great offense; but to cast consecrated bread to dogs is a grievous sin.

7. This sin was accompanied with diverse monstrous sins; first, horrible doubting of God's truth: secondly, compacting with God's utter enemy, and so making apostasy from God to the devil: thirdly, consent to the blasphemies of the devil, when he spoke enviously, and scoffingly at God: fourthly, affectation of divinity: fifthly, a wretchless disregard

of what should become of his posterity, through his venturous course: with many other sins.

2. For the second, God was just in deriving this loss to their posterity: for Adam was the common root of all mankind, and we were in his loins, as Levi was in Abraham's, when he paid tithes; and are traitors not punished in their children? The acts of a burgess in the Parliament is the act of the country.

Objection. But yet at least godly men should not beget ungodly children.

Answer. They beget children, as men, not as godly men; I mean, they derive such a nature as they have, which is corrupt after their calling: though they are justified perfectly, yet they are sanctified but in part: The father that was circumcised begat a child that was uncircumcised; and take the cleanest corn in the world, and sow it, and it brings forth chaff in the ear itself with the corn. In this way we have considered this for information sake.

The doctrine of the fall may also serve for instruction; and so both in general and particular.

1. In general it should teach us four things:

1. First, to take heed of the fountains of all apostasy. There were three things occasioned mightily concerning the fall of our first parents:

The first was a rebellious desire to be what God would not have us to be.

The second, unthankfulness: all the pleasures of paradise will not please them, if they are crossed in just one thing, no matter how small that thing might be.

Third, the liberty they took to add or detract from God's word: they added the word *touch*, and they detracted, when they say, "lest ye die:" and these three sins are, and ever will be, causes of apostasy; if they are not prevented.

2. Secondly, let us be warned here, that while we live, to keep out of the company of such as fall away from the truth, as the devil did. All apostates are like the devil; they will not be quiet until they make others fall away with them.

3. Thirdly, we should forever be warned here to look to ourselves, and make our conscience even of the lesser sins. We see here what the eating of an apple did, which most men would gladly think was but a small matter; and rather, because monstrous sins may be committed about a small offense in itself, this we should consider. Think of the man that gathered sticks on the Sabbath day who was stoned to death, and of the case of Ananias and Sapphira for keeping back a little profit from the sale of their land.

4. We must get on our armor, and make all provision we can against the devil. We see here how he thirsts after the ruin of man; and if he prevailed so over Adam, how much more easily may he prevail over us? and if he could deceive by the means of a serpent there; how much more now, when he speaks to us by men like ourselves? Yes, then we saw a proof of it, for how quickly was Adam enticed when the devil spoke to him in the mouth of Eve, his wife.

And here we may observe the devil's method in tempting, and the degrees of temptation: For there was:

1. First, the suggestion itself.

2. The obscuring of the thoughts about eminency of God, and the excellency of the image received of him.

3. An impression of forgetfulness in the memory, not distinctly remembering what was before done, or commanded of God.

4. The tickling of ambition, affecting to be more than they were.

5. Trust given to the flatteries and baits of the devil, and a contracted familiarity with him, with inclination of the will and affection to the prohibited fruit. So much for this in general.

2. In particular, four sorts must be warned:

1. First, women should here be very humbled, and forever be mistrustful of their counsels, and carriage: for Satan knows how to make use of them *still*.

2. Secondly, men must take heed of whisperings, and enticing advice of women.

3. Thirdly, the weak must carefully look to themselves, that Satan not employ them as instruments of temptation; and they should learn not to be so violent in things they are not fully grounded in.

4. The strong must take heed lest they fall. If Adam fell in paradise, they are in more danger now in the world; neither may they trust in their own gifts, but learn to place all their trust in God.

5. As any are more godly, so they must know they shall be more assaulted. So much for instruction in this.

This doctrine of the fall has a matter in it of extreme humiliation, in that eternal shame lies on our nature by this vile offense, both in respect of the extremity of our loss, and the fearful displeasure of God.

Lastly, it may comfort the godly to think of their estate by Christ, having received the assurance of a better condition, than they ever could have had in Adam; and rather, because they are now confirmed as the angels of heaven, that they can never fall from the happiness they have in Christ.

CHAPTER 9:
Of Sin

"Wherefore, as by one man sin entered into the world, and death by sin; and so death went over all men; forasmuch as all men have sinned," (Romans 5:12).

We find here the *cause* of our misery. The parts to follow are sin and punishment.

1. The principles concerning sin are,

1. First, that all men have sinned, "The fool hath said in his heart, there is no God: they have corrupted and done an abominable work; there is none that doth good. The Lord looked down from heaven upon the children of men, to see if there were any that would understand and seek God. All are gone out of the way, they are all corrupt, there is none that doth good, no not one," (Psalm 14:1-3). "Who can say I have made mine heart clean? I am clean from my sin?" (Proverbs 20:9). "There is no man that sinneth not," (Ecclesiastes 7:22). "What then, are we more excellent? No in no wise: for we have already proved that all both Jews and Gentiles are under sin," (Romans 3:9). "For in many things we sin all," (James 3:2). "If we say that we have no sin, we deceive ourselves, and the truth is not in us," (1 John 1:8).

2. The second principle is, that the nature of man is stained with sin from birth, "Who can bring a clean thing out of filthiness? There is not one," (Job 14:4). "What is man that he should be clean? And he that is born of a woman that he should be just?" (Job 15:14). "Behold I was born in iniquity, and in sin hath my mother conceived me," (Psalm 51:5).

3. That this infection has overspread the whole nature of man, here called *the old man*. For explanation of this principle, we must consider that the nature of man is tainted in 14 ways: For there is in man by nature:

1. Extreme darkness, sightless, especially in the knowledge of God and happiness. "Who hath delivered us from the power of darkness," (Colossians 1:13). "But the natural man perceiveth not the things of the Spirit of God, for they are foolishness unto him; neither can he know them, because they are spiritually discerned," (1 Corinthians 2:14).

2. Insensibleness, and unutterable hardness of heart, "Having their cogitation darkened, and being strangers from the life of God, through the ignorance that is in them, because of the hardness of their heart," (Ephesians 4:18).

3. Impotency, and extreme disability to deliver our own souls, or break off our sins, "He feedeth of ashes; a seduced heart hath deceived him, that he cannot deliver his soul, nor say, is there not a lie in my right hand?" (Isaiah 44:20).

4. Enmity to that which is good, "For the wisdom of the flesh is enmity to God," (Romans 8:7). "But I see another law in my members, rebelling against the law of my mind, and leading me captive unto the law of sin, which is in my members," (Romans 7:23).

5. Impurity, foulness, filthiness, all over, "Unto them that are defiled and unbelieving, is nothing pure, for even their minds and conscience are defiled," (Titus 1:15). "All are gone out of the way, they are all corrupt, there is none that doth good, no not one," (Psalm 14:3).

6. Abundance of false principles.

7. Proneness to all sorts of evil, "For we know that the law is spiritual, but I am carnal, sold under sin. I find then by

the law, that when I would do good, evil is present with me," (Romans 7:14, 21). Concupiscence.

8. Lack of all righteousness, defects of the love, fear, and joy in God: so also of mercy, "All are gone out of the way, they are all corrupt, there is none that doth good, no not one," (Psalm 14:3). "As it is written, there is none righteous, no not one," (Romans 3:10).

9. The members are naturally servants of sin: so are the senses, "Neither give you your members as weapons of unrighteousness unto sin. Know ye not, that to whomsoever ye give yourselves as servants to obey, his servants you are to whom ye obey; whether it be of sin unto death, or of obedience unto righteousness," (Romans 6:13-16).

10. A servile will, a will that apprehends no liberty but in sinning, (Romans 7:14).

11. A natural aptness to be scandalized, so as Christ himself is an offense: a rock of offense, (1 Corinthians 8:7; 2 Peter 2:6).

12. A natural savoring and relishing of the things of Satan, "Wherein in time past you walked according to the course of this world, and after the prince that ruleth the air, even the spirit that now worketh in the children of disobedience?" (Ephesians 2:2). This has been ever since the first temptation in paradise.

13. Corruption of memory. Forgetting good. Retaining evil.

14. A natural disunion from one another, lusts of disagreement, shunning all hearty communion with others through dislike, and self-love, "From whence are wars and contentions amongst you? Are they not hence, even of your lusts that fight in your members," (James 4:1).

These things prove that we have all vile natures, that there is not one of a good nature in the world by nature.

4. The fourth principle is that besides these sins that stick fast upon our natures, every man is guilty of horrible, many, and vile actual sins, "They have corrupted and done an abominable work," (Psalm 14:1-3). "Behold he found no steadfastness in his saints: yea the heavens are not clean in his sight. How much more is man abominable and filthy, who drinketh iniquity like water," (Job 15:15-16). "They have all gone out of the way," (Romans 3:12). Such as are,

1. A world of evil thoughts, "When the Lord saw that the wickedness of man was great in the earth, and all the imaginations of the thoughts of his heart were only evil continually," (Genesis 6:5). Atheistic thoughts, impure thoughts, vain thoughts, are all innumerable.

2. Vile affections: Impatience, lust, anger, envy, suspicion, malice, worldly fear, trust, joy, love, *etc.*

3. Vile words: bitter, idle, false, flattering, slandering, proud, filthy, deceitful, scornful, censuring words.

4. Atheistic works, (Psalm 14:1,3) as in many places before. Against God's worship in all the parts. Against the Sabbath. In our particular and general calling. At home and abroad. Secret and open. Of omission and commission. Of ignorance and knowledge. Of a sudden and of custom. In company and out of company. Hypocrisy, pride, security, unbelief, impenitence. In prosperity and adversity. Partaking with other's sin. Our own righteousness, as "is as filthy rags, and we all do fade like a leaf, and our iniquities like the wind have taken us away," (Isaiah 64:6).

Besides personal faults, as drunkenness, usury, swearing, whoredom, works of the flesh, "Moreover the works of the flesh are manifest, which are adultery, fornication, uncleanness, wantonness," (Galatians 5:19-21).

The uses of these principles are fourfold.

1. First for information, and that in nine things. For by this we may know:

1. That there can be no justification by our works, "Therefore by the works of the law shall no flesh be justified in his sight; for by the law cometh the knowledge of sin," (Romans 9:20). "If thou (O Lord) straitly markest iniquities, (O Lord) who shall stand?" (Psalm 130:3). For every mouth must be stopped, and all the world be guilty before God.

2. That the cause of all God's disregard of us, and the miseries that befell us, is in ourselves. How can we murmur at our crosses, if we look on our sins? There is mercy in the greatest judgment; for it is his mercy that we are not consumed, "It is the Lord's mercy that we are not consumed, because his compassions fail not," (Lamentations 3:22). If Adam's one sin deserved it, what do all these in us deserve?

3. That it will never go well with the wicked, though God forbears for a long time, "Because sentence against an evil work is not executed speedily: therefore the heart of the children of men is fully set to do evil. But it shall not be well to the wicked, neither shall he prolong his days; he shall be like a shadow, because he feareth not before God," (Ecclesiastes 8:11-12).

4. That no man has cause to brag of his good nature, there are so many springs of sin within us.

5. That the things that defile a man, are from within, in himself, it is not any outward deformity, ill clothes, or natural foulness.

6. That *a little repentance* will not serve the turn.

7. That there is a difference between the wicked and the godly in sinning.

8. Concerning God's providence in the death of infants: we kill young snakes and adders, because they will sting, as well as the old, because they have stung.

9. Do not say, God is the cause of our ruin; nor is it your chance, or ill luck, or only the devil that brought you into this or that mischief. It is your own ill nature.

2. Secondly, for humiliation:

First to the godly in two respects:

1. Because they find so many of their old corruptions, having received such graces and mercies from God.

2. Because they yet are the means of the conveyance of original sin to their children.

Secondly, to such wicked men as live in open sins, yet do not repent. Why do their hearts carry them away? (Job 15:12,14).

Do the workers of iniquity have no knowledge? Are they guilty of so many reasons, and fallen into the hands of a righteous judge, and yet secure? "They know not and understand nothing, they walk in darkness, albeit all the foundations of the earth be moved," (Psalm 82:5).

To civil honest men: for here they may learn how vile their estate is, though God has restrained some evils in them, *for:*

1. They lack the image of God.

2. They have an infected nature in all the former fourteen things.

3. There is in them a disability in the manner of all holy duties.

4. They partake of other men's sins many ways.

5. They are guilty of many omissions.

6. They abound in inward sins, by which God is vexed, as, "When the Lord saw that the wickedness of man was great in the earth, and all the imaginations of the thoughts of his heart were only evil continually," (Genesis 6:5); and Satan by them can set upon strongholds, (2 Corinthians 10:5).

7. They are guilty of many outward evils against the least commandments.

3. The third use is for instruction, and so strong Christians should learn to admire and praise God,

1. That could be pacified. O what is man, that God should here look on such a dunghill!

2. That has so promised to make us clean in part from such filthiness, taking away the body of sins, and seasoning the fountain, and drying it up.

2. Secondly, weak Christians should never be at rest, until they get assurance of their pardon in the blood of Jesus Christ.

3. Thirdly, all the *godly:*

1. Should strive after the contrary holiness, and to express the reformation of their natures and lives, "and cast off concerning the conversation in times past, the old man, which is corrupt through the deceivable lusts," (Ephesians 4:22).

2. Should walk humbly all their days, because of the many remainders of corruption, as, "For I allow not that which I do: for what I would, that I do not: but what I hate, that do I," (Romans 7:15-16) and look to their hearts, "Taking heed lest at any time there be in any of them an evil heart, and unfaithful to depart away from the living God," (Hebrews 3:12).

3. It should work in all the godly a wonderful desire of final redemption, "O wretched man that I am, who shall deliver me from the body of this death!" (Romans 7:24). "O give salvation unto Israel out of Zion, when the Lord turneth the

captivity of his people, then Jacob shall rejoice, and Israel shall be glad," (Psalm 14:7).

O how should we desire to get out of the world! Seeing all so leprous, the plague forerunning upon every man, so as we are in danger to be infected in all places, and by all persons.

4. It should work in wicked men a fervent desire of remission, and constant endeavor in the confession of sin, crying out daily with the leper, "unclean, unclean."

4. The last use is for consolation.

1. First, to all men for the Lord uses this, as an argument of pity and mercy, "And the lord smelled a savor of rest, and the Lord said in his heart, I will henceforth curse the ground no more for man's cause: for the imaginations of man's heart is evil even from his youth, neither will I smite anymore all things living, as I have done," (Genesis 8:21). "I knew that thou wouldest grievously transgress; therefore have I called thee a transgressor from thy womb: yet for my namesake I will defer," (Isaiah 48:8-9) "Then hear thou in heaven their prayer, and their supplication, and judge their cause: If they sin against thee (for there is no man that sinneth not), and thou be angry with them, and deliver them unto the enemies, and they take them away captive unto a land far and near," (2 Chronicles 6:35-36).

2. To the godly: they should admiringly rejoice in their privilege in the blood of Christ, and in the remission of all their sins.

CHAPTER 10:
Of Punishment of Sin

"Wherefore as by one man sin entered into the world, and death by sin: and so death went over all men, forasmuch as all men have sinned," (Romans 5:12).

Here are the principles concerning sin. Now concerning the punishment of sin, follows this principle, *viz. That all men in their natural estate are extremely miserable, in respect of the punishment, to which they are liable for their sins.*

"God is jealous, and the Lord revengeth, even the Lord of anger, the Lord will take vengeance on his adversaries, and he reserveth wrath for his enemies. The Lord is slow to anger: but he is great in power, and will not surely clear the wicked: the Lord hath his way in the whirlwind, and in the storm, and the clouds are the dust of his feet. Who can stand before his wrath, or who can abide in the fierceness of his wrath? His wrath is poured out like fire, and the rocks are broken by him," (Nahum 1:2-3,6). "Thou renewest thy plagues against me, and thou increasest thy wrath against me: changes and armies of sorrows are against me," (Romans 5:12, Job 10:17). "Is not destruction to the wicked, and strange punishments to the workers of iniquity?" (Job 31:3). "Which shall be punished with everlasting perdition from the presence of the Lord, and from the glory of his power," (2 Thessalonians 1:9). "Among whom we also had our conversation in times past in the lusts of our flesh, in fulfilling the will of the flesh and of the mind, and were by nature the children of wrath, as well as others," (Ephesians 2:3).

That this principle may be explained, I will reckon up the several sorts of punishments, which have been inflicted for man's sin.

1. The loss of paradise, from which we are all exiled, so as we live as banished men, while we are in this world, "Thus he cast out man, and at the east side of the Garden of Eden he set the cherubim, and the blade of a sword shaken, to keep the way of the tree of life," (Genesis 3:24).

2. The curse of the creatures: the creatures are subject to vanity, and subdued to bondage, under which they groan for man's sin, "Because the creature is subject to vanity, not of its own will, but by reason of him which hath subdued it under hope," (Romans 8:20-21). "Cursed is the earth for thy sake, in sorrow shalt thou eat of it all the days of thy life. Thorns also and thistles shall it bring forth unto thee, and thou shalt eat the herb of the field," (Genesis 3:17-18).

3. An impure and painful birth, "Unto the woman he said, I will greatly increase thy sorrows, and thy conceptions: in sorrow shalt thou bring forth children; and thy desires shall be subject to thy husband, and he shall rule over thee," (Genesis 3:16).

4. The displeasure of God, and his fearful anger conceived against us, "He that obeyeth not the Son shall not see life, but the wrath of God abideth on him," (John 3:36). "And I will cast filth upon thee, and make thee vile, and will set thee as a gazing stock," (Nahum 3:6).

5. A privation of that admirable knowledge of God, and the nature of the creatures, to which we were created; so as we are all for horrible ignorance almost like the beasts, in comparison of what once we might have had, "Surely I am more foolish than any man, and have not the understanding of a man

in me," (Proverbs 30:2): and this light is wanting both to the mind and the conscience.

6. Bondage to Satan, who naturally has strongholds in every man's heart, and such spiritual possession that having men in his snare, he leads them at his pleasure, and works effectually both in them, and by them, "Wherein in time past you walked according to the course of this world, and after the prince that ruleth in the air, even the spirit that now worketh in the children of disobedience," (Ephesians 2:2). "And that they may come to amendment out of the snare of the devil, which are taken of him at his will," (2 Timothy 2:26). "Casting down the imaginations, and every high thing that is exalted against the knowledge of God," (2 Corinthians 10:5).

7. Spiritual death, which comprehends in it the loss of communion with God (the life of our lives), and all the joys of his favor and presence, together with the obduration of our hearts, which are become as a stone within us; so as we are altogether insensible of the things that concern everlasting happiness. "And you hath he quickened, that were dead in trespasses and sins," (Ephesians 2:1). "Having their cogitation darkened, and being strangers from the life of God, through the ignorance that is in them, because of the hardness of their heart," (Ephesians 4:18). "I will take away the stony heart out of your body, and I will give you a heart of flesh," (Ezekiel 36:26).

8. Miserable bodies. Our bodies have become miserable, both in respect of deformity, and in respect of imbecility; as also in respect of the many pains that befall them, both from labor, and from diseases of all sorts. "In the sweat of thy face shalt thou eat bread, till thou return to the earth: for out of it wast thou taken, because thou art dust, and to dust shalt thou return," (Genesis 3:13). "The Lord shall make the pestilence

cleave unto thee, until he hath consumed thee from the land, whither thou goest to possess it. The Lord shall smite thee with a consumption, and with the fever, and with a, extreme burning, and with fervent heat, and with the sword, and with blasting, and with the mildew, and they shall pursue thee, until thou perish," (Deuteronomy 28:21-22).

9. Judgments in our outward estates in temporal things by wars, famine, fire, earthquakes, inundations, ignominy, poverty, and such like of many sorts, "Cursed shalt thou be in the town, and cursed also in the field: Cursed shall thy basket be, and thy dough: Cursed shall be the fruit of thy body, and the fruit of thy land, the increase of thy kin, and the stocks of thy sheep: Cursed shalt thou be when thou comest in, and cursed also when thou goest out," (Deuteronomy 28:16-18).

10. The restraining of good things from us, even blessings of all sorts; and that sometimes when they are by the free mercy of God bestowed upon others, "But your iniquities have separated between you and your God, and your sins have hid his face from you, that he will not hear," (Isaiah 59:2). "For what portion should I have of God from above? And what inheritance of the Almighty from on high?" (Job 31:2). "And the time of this ignorance God regarded not," (Acts 17:30). "Yet your iniquities have turned away these things, and your sins have hindered good things from you," (Jeremiah 5:25).

11. The cursing of blessings, when God blasts the good gifts he bestowed, or suffers prosperity to become a snare, or trap, or ruin unto man, "I will curse your blessings," (Malachi 2:2). "They have sown wheat, and reaped thorns, they have put themselves to much pain, and had no profit: and they shall be ashamed of their revenues, because of the fierce wrath of the Lord," (Jeremiah 12:13). "Let their table be a snare before them, and their prosperity their ruin," (Psalm 69:22). "I will also laugh

at your destruction, and mock when your fear cometh," (Proverbs 1:26).

12. Scourging of sin with sin, which is one of the most grievous punishments; when God leaves a man so, as he suffers him to fall into scandalous courses, and to commit sin with greediness; or delivers man up to a reprobate mind, "For this cause God gave them up unto vile affections; for even their women did change the natural use, into that, which is against nature. For as they regarded not to know God, even so God delivered them up unto a reprobate mind, to do those things which are not convenient," (Romans 1:26,28).

13. Hellish terrors, which wound the soul with insupportable torments, many times God softening the heart to feel inward pain, or suffering Satan to torment the soul with unspeakable fears and horrors, "But a fearful looking for of judgment and violent fire, which shall devour the adversaries," (Hebrews 10:27). "The sinners in Zion are afraid, a fear is come upon the hypocrites, who among us shall dwell with the devouring fire? Who among us shall dwell with the everlasting burnings?" (Isaiah 33:14). "Therefore thus saith the Lord, behold my servants shall eat, and ye shall be hungry; behold my servants shall drink, and ye shall be thirsty; behold my servants shall rejoice, and ye shall be ashamed. Behold my servants shall sing for joy of heart, and ye shall cry for sorrow of heart, and shall howl for vexation of mind," (Isaiah 65:13-14).

14. Fear of death, which in some measure is in all, though the former is not; every man being in that respect like a prisoner that is condemned, and looks every day when he shall go to execution, "And that he might deliver all them, which for fear of death were all their lifetime subject to change," (Hebrews 2:15).

15. A terrible general judgment, when all men's sins shall be ripped up before the whole world, to their eternal shame; and an order given for unavoidable execution of the sentence, "Because he hath appointed a day, in the which he will judge the world in righteousness, by that man, whom he hath appointed," (Acts 17:31).

16. A miserable departure, and loss of life, the soul and body being rent asunder, and both losing forever all the pleasures, or felicities of this life; "Wherefore as by one man sin entered into the world, and death by sin; and so death went over all men, forasmuch as all men have sinned," (Romans 5:12). "For the wages of sin is death," (Romans 6:23).

17. Lastly, eternal pain. Now this eternal misery is lamentable, if we consider, 1. either its degrees; 2. or the place: 3. or its continuance.

The degrees of damnation are;

1. First, they have no communion with God, nor participation in any of the blessings of God, "Which shall be punished with everlasting perdition from the presence of the Lord, and from the glory of his power," (2 Thessalonians 1:9).

2. Secondly, they are united to the devil, with whom they have an eternal fearful fellowship, "Then shall he say unto them on the left hand; depart from me ye cursed into everlasting fire, which is prepared for the devil and his angels," (Matthew 25:41).

3. They endure an unspeakable confusion, and most bitter ignominy, on the consideration of the discovery of their many shameful offenses.

4. They are inwardly affected with incredible horror, and torment of conscience, arising from the sense of God's anger for their sins, "For Tophet is prepared of old; it is even prepared for the King; he hath made it deep and large; the

burning thereof is fire and much wood, the breath of the Lord, like a river of brimstone doth kindle it," (Isaiah 30:33). "But unto them that are contentious and disobey the truth, and obey unrighteousness, shall be indignation and wrath. Tribulation and anguish shall be upon the soul of every man that doth evil: of the Jew first, and also of the Grecian," (Romans 2:8-9).

5. The bodies of the damned shall suffer inexpressible torments, which is set out in Scriptures by their lying in fire and brimstone, (Isaiah 30:33) as immediately before. "And being in hell torments, he lifted up his eyes, and saw Abraham afar off, and Lazarus in his bosom," (Luke 16:23). "But the fearful and unbelieving, and the abominable, and murderers, and whoremongers, and sorcerers, and idolaters, and all liars, shall have their part in the lake which burneth with fire and brimstone, which is the second death," (Revelation 21:8). "Then shall he say unto them on the left hand, depart from me ye cursed into everlasting fire, which is prepared for the devil and his angels," (Matthew 25:41).

This misery is increased by the fearfulness of the place where it is to be suffered, to which in diverse Scriptures, diverse names are given to intimate its horror, and "Hell, the pit, the great deep, or bottomless gulf, prison, darkness, utter darkness," and many other terrible titles.

"Then said the King to his servants, bind him hand and foot; take him away, and cast him into utter darkness, there shall be weeping and gnashing of teeth," (Matthew 22:13). "And I saw an Angel come down from heaven, having the key of the bottomless pit, and a great chain in his hand," (Revelation 20:1).

And all this the more miserable because it shall be both eternal, and without intermission, or ease, "And the smoke of their torment shall ascend evermore, and they shall have no rest day nor night," (Revelation 14:11). Now follow the uses.

1. The use may be first for singular reproof of the marvelous security of multitudes of people, that can live quietly in so miserable a condition; were not man sunk deep into rebellion, and soiled with unspeakable senselessness, one would think it were impossible for him to eat, sleep, or ever to hold up his head. If we heard a story of the one half of these distresses that were befallen another man, and laid our hearts to it to think tenderly of it, we should not but wonder, that that man could so forget his own safety, as to neglect any means for his own release? But this very observation shows two things, *viz.* that men are guilty of vile atheism, and unbelief, and of incredible apathy, or insensibleness. O that men would but think of these particulars, and ponder them seriously! But alas, a deceived heart has seduced them, that they cannot say, *here is my perdition, if I do not repent.* And this reproof is aggravated against some men in this, that they are angry at any that shows them their danger, as we see by experience of men, that live in gross sins. Yet, let the curses due to those sins be applied to them, how do they rage? How are they like the very horse and mule, and much worse?

2. Secondly, here is a matter of instruction, and that first to wicked men, that (if it is possible) they would awake from this heavy sleep in sin,[8] and learn to live righteously. These judgments[9] may warn all men everywhere to repent: and seeing they are thus undone by the first Adam,[10] to seek release from

---

[8] Ephesians 5:14.
[9] 1 Corinthians 15; Acts 17:31.
[10] Romans 5:12.

this dreadful misery by the second Adam; [11] There is no condemnation to them that are in Christ Jesus; and there can be no access to Christ[12] without repentance from dead works, and faith in him. O how were men sure to be freed by Christ, if they were once weary and heavy laden! There is a full propitiation for all sin in him; he has born all that curse of the law, only if any man will be in Christ he must be a new creature.

This may instruct the godly, and so,

1. The weak Christian should labor by all means to be established in the faith, that as Christ has freed him from all these miseries (as curses), so faith may free him from the fear of them; and to this end he should earnestly and constantly pray that "God would make him worthy of his calling, and fulfill all the good pleasure of his goodness, and the work of faith with power," (2 Thessalonians 1:11-12).

2. All Christians should forcibly compel on themselves a careful practice of 6 duties:

1. All ages should admire the, "exceeding riches of the tender kindness and mercy of God, and the great love wherewith he hath loved us," that has forgiven us so great a debt, and freed us from such an unspeakable confusion, (Ephesians 2:4, 7).

2. We should often look on Christ, that has born all the malediction of the law for us, and that both to move us to compassion, and mourning for our sins, that so pierced him, (Zechariah 12:10). And also to settle ourselves against the fear of any of these miseries, seeing Christ has fully paid our debts, and suffered the uttermost in our stead. And further, if we did often set before us that marvelous passion of our Lord and

---

[11] Romans 5:1, Matthew 11:29.

[12] 1 John 2:1, Galatians 3:13, 2 Corinthians 5:17.

Savior, it might ravish our hearts to a greater love towards him and desire to be with him to give him eternal thanks.

3. Have we escaped so much danger, which sin brought us into? Then let us forever be warned, and go our ways, and sin no more. Let us watch over ourselves, that we are not bewitched by the deceitfulness of sin. For here we may learn that God can make sin extremely bitter to us, but especially let us leave sin, even because God has dealt so graciously with us.

4. It should teach us with all compassion to pity others with whom we converse, that yet live in this misery, we should strive with all effectualness of persuasion to draw them out of such an estate, and use our uttermost power to pull them out of this fire, provoking them to holiness, and good works, and exhorting and rebuking them with all instance, that they may not perish in so great condemnation, (Hebrews 10:25).

5. It should teach us to endure all sorts of afflictions. God shall please to try us with it, and that because they are no way comparable to the punishments we are escaped from. And besides, God is pleased to cause them to work for our good. They try and increase our faith in Christ's merits. They make us know ourselves more thoroughly. They mollify and soften our hearts. They tame our flesh. They scour our gifts from rust. They wean us from the world, and excite the desire after, and care to provide for the world to come.

6. It should teach us with all gladness of heart to remember our miseries, as waters that are past, and establish ourselves in a daily solace, especially in the expectation of the full and final deliverance from all the remnants of distress in the day of Christ, when God, "shall be made marvelous in them that believe," (2 Thessalonians 1:11). And the more we should lift up our heads, on whom the ends of the world are come, because the day of that redemption draws near. Let us ever say with

David, "The lines are fallen upon me in pleasant places: yea I have a fair heritage," (Psalm 16:6); and, "The Lord hath drawn us out of many waters," (Psalm 22:24). Let us, therefore, love the Lord dearly, and rejoice always in the Lord, (Philippians 4:4).

CHAPTER 11:
The Estate of Grace

"As he hath chosen us in him before the foundation of the world," (Ephesians 1:4).

Here now we have finished the second estate of man. The third estate is the estate of grace, which is to be considered in three ways:

1. First, in respect of the means of its foundation.

2. Secondly, in respect of the subject of its possession, which is the Church.

3. Thirdly, in respect of the degrees of application, and manifestation, which are two:

1. Justification

2. Sanctification

1. The means of the foundation is twofold:

1. Election in God

2. Redemption in Christ

1. First, that there was a choice and election made by God, "As he hath chosen us in him, before the foundation of the world," (Ephesians 1:4).

2. Secondly, that this choice was before the foundation of the world, (Ephesians 1:4) as immediately before, "(For the children being not yet born, neither having done any good or evil, that the purpose of God according to election might stand, not of works, but of him that calleth)," (Romans 9:11).

3. That only some men are chosen, not all men. If all were taken, how could there be an *election?* "Many are called, but few are chosen," (Matthew 20:16, 22:14).

4. That the cause of our election is the only free grace of God, not our works, "Who hath predestined us, to be adopted through Jesus Christ unto himself, according to the good pleasure of his will," (Ephesians 1:5). "For he saith unto Moses; I will have mercy on him, to whom I will show mercy: and will have compassion on him, on whom I will have compassion. Therefore hath he mercy on whom he will have mercy, and whom he will, he hardeneth," (Romans 9:15, 18).

5. That God's election is unchangeable, and all the elect shall be saved, "Moreover, whom he predestinated, them also he called; and whom he called, them also he justified; and whom he justified, them also he glorified," (Romans 8:30). "My counsel shall stand, and I will do whatsoever I will," (Isaiah 46:8-10). "But the foundation of God remaineth sure, and hath this seal; The Lord knoweth who are his," (2 Timothy 2:19). "All that the Father giveth me shall come to me; and him that cometh to me, I cast not away," (John 6:37). "Then shall the King say to them on the right hand, Come ye blessed of my Father; inherit the kingdom prepared for you from the foundations of the world," (Matthew 25:34).

The consideration of this doctrine of man's election should teach us diverse things:

1. Every one of us should study this doctrine of our election, and labor to make it sure, seeing here lies the foundation of our grace. Now, one labor we have accomplishes both, for if we make our calling sure, we make our election sure, (2 Peter 1:10). And we may be sure our calling is right, if we add virtue to our faith, if we can find the gifts of grace in our hearts: for this (I say) we must study the doctrine of the signs; of which I said this before.

2. If we find assurance of our election, we should with all thankfulness acknowledge God's goodness to us, and the

riches of his free grace, as the Apostle teaches us, "But we ought to give thanks always to the Lord for you brethren, beloved of God, because God hath from the beginning chosen you to salvation, through justification of the Spirit, and the faith of truth," (Ephesians 1:3; 2 Thessalonians 2:13): and so rest in this happiness, as our chief desire to God should be still to vouchsafe us this favor to bless us with the favor of his chosen, "Remember me, O Lord, with the favor of thy people, visit me with thy salvation. "That I may see the felicity of thy chosen, and rejoice in the joy of thy people, and glory with thine inheritance," (Psalm 106:4-5).

And forever stand and gaze at the marvelous riches of God's grace, that suffered us not to perish in the condemnation of the world.

3. Our election should work on us a wonderful care of holiness of life. Are we elect? Then how should we confirm ourselves in separation from the world? Shall we ever love the world and the things of it, and hear that God has chosen us *out* of the world? Yes, why do we fashion ourselves to this world? "And fashion not yourselves like unto this world, but be ye changed by the renewing of your mind, that ye may prove what is the good will of God, and acceptable, and perfect," (Romans 12:2). "For thou art an holy people unto the Lord thy God, and the Lord hath chosen thee to be a precious people unto himself above all the people that are upon the earth," (Deuteronomy 14:2).

God has chosen us, and called us with a holy calling; and therefore we should as a people peculiar to him, be zealous of all good works, and show forth the virtues of him that called us, and walk before him with all desire to please him, that has in this way elected us; we should ever be ready to choose the Lord to be our God, and to show it by promising ourselves to him, and by walking in his ways, as these Scriptures plentifully show. "For thou art an holy people unto the Lord thy God, the Lord thy God hath chosen thee to be a precious people unto himself, above all the people that are upon the earth. The Lord doth not set his love upon you, nor choose you, because ye were more in number than any people: for ye were the fewest of all people," (Deuteronomy 7:6-7). "This day the Lord thy God hath commanded thee to do these ordinances and laws, keep them therefore, and do them with all thine heart, and with all thy soul. Thou hast set up the Lord this day to be thy God, and to walk in his ways, and to keep his ordinances, and his commandments, and his laws, and to hearken to his voice," (Deuteronomy 26:16-17). "As he hath chosen us in him before the foundation of the world, that we should be holy, and without blame before him in love," (Ephesians 1:4). "But ye are a chosen generation, a royal priesthood, an holy nation, a peculiar people, that ye should shew forth the virtues of him, that hath called you out of darkness into his marvelous light. As free, and not as having the liberty for a cloak of maliciousness, but as the servants of God," (1 Peter 2:9, 16).

We should give our names to God, as those that will subscribe and devote themselves only to the God of Jacob, "Yet now hear, O Jacob, my servant, and Israel, whom I have chosen. One shall say, I am the Lord; another shall be called by the name of Jacob; and another shall subscribe with his hand unto the Lord, and name himself by the name of Israel," (Isaiah 44:1, 5).

4. It should teach us to imitate God, and choose the godly, as the persons we would most observe, admire, love, defend, and live with, "These things command I you, that ye love one another," (John 15:17). "And I have declared unto them thy name, and will declare it, that the love wherewith thou hast loved me, may be in them, and I in them," (John 17:26). Yes, we

should not have the glorious faith of Christ, in respect of people to despise poor Christians, and only respect great men. For, God has chosen the weak things of this world to confound the mighty, and the poor he has chosen to be made heirs of the kingdom, and rich in faith, (James 2:15, 1 Corinthians 1:17). Yes, we should be content, as the Apostle says, to suffer all things for the elect's sake, seeing they are so dear to God, (2 Timothy 2:10).

We may know our election by two sorts of signs. First, the one respects God. Secondly, the other respects ourselves. God declares his eternal choice by diverse marks of it, and man proves himself to be elect of God by diverse tokens of it.

God shows whom he has chosen from everlasting in three manners of ways:

1. By election in time, when God separates a man from the world to himself and his service. It is a manifest sign of election. It shows an eternal choice, when God singles a man out from the multitude of carnal and careless men, and inspires him with an unchangeable resolution to devote himself to God. It is an evident declaration of God's predestination to glory; God separates a man from the world, when he makes him weary of wicked and unprofitable society; and takes away from him the taste in earthly things, so as the love of the world is not in him, and sanctifies him to his own use.

2. By the entertainment God gives them in his house, and especially by the efficacy of the word, and principally by the life of the promises. For, God makes his word a word of power, and the Holy Spirit falls on their hearts, and they at sometimes feel a marvelous assurance in hearing, and so much comfort, that they can receive the word, though it is with much affliction, and rejoice greatly in it; and the world transforms them also to a constant desire of practice and imitation of the

godliness of the saints, "Knowing, beloved brethren, that ye are elect of God: For our Gospel was not unto you in word only, but also in power, and in the Holy Ghost, and in much assurance: And ye became followers of us, and of the Lord, and received the word in much affliction, with joy of the Holy Ghost," (1 Thessalonians 1:4-6). "Blessed is he whom thou choosest, and causest to come to thee, he shall dwell in thy courts, and we shall be satisfied with the pleasures of thine house even thy holy temple," (Psalm 65:4). "That is, they which are the children of the flesh, are not the children of God: but the children of promise are counted for the seed," (Romans 9:8, 11).

3. By the sanctification of their afflictions, even by the many experiences of God's love in afflictions, as when God comforts their hearts in the midst of distress, when they come to him, making their moan; and when he turns the cross to a blessing to them, making them more humble by it, exercising their gifts, purging out their sin, and at the length giving gracious deliverances, causing all to work together for the best, so as they themselves being judges, they can say that it was good for them, that they were afflicted, "Also we know that all things work together for the good of those that love God, even to them that are called of his purpose," (Romans 8:28). See also Psalm 119 in many places.

Now as God manifests his own choice by these and other of the same signs, so the godly make sure of their own election by diverse marks, as generally by the sanctification of the Spirit, and belief of the truth, "But we ought to give thanks always to God for you brethren, beloved of the Lord, because that God hath chosen you to salvation through the sanctification of the Spirit, and the faith of truth," (2 Thessalonians 2:13). So in particular:

1. By the virtues of Christ, which more or less in some measure shine in them, such as are, "humility, piety, knowledge, temperance, and contempt of the world, patience in adversity," and other excellent saving graces in them, (2 Peter 1:5-7, 10; 1 Peter 2:9). By their fruits you may know them, (John 15:16).

2. Secondly, by the affections of godliness, that are in them above all others, (Ephesians 1:5; 1 John 3:14). They approve themselves to be elect by love; that is, by their great affections to God, to the word of God, and his ordinances, and by their brotherly kindness to the godly, and this love is the more evident mark, when it lasts even in affliction, when no distresses makes us abate of our affection to God, or good things, or good men, (Romans 8:28).

3. By their priesthood. God's elect are a kingdom of priests, they offer God daily sacrifice, they have the spirit of prayer, and they daily mortify *the beast of their sins* on the altar of Christ crucified. So then by their praying and their mortification, God's elect may be evidently known, (1 Peter 2:9-10).

4. Fourthly, they are usually known by the opposition of the world. If they were of the world, the world would spare, and love his own. But because they are chosen out of the world, therefore the world hates them, and pursues them with reproaches, and indignations of all sorts, "If the world hates you, you know that it hated me before you. If ye were of the world, the world would love his own: but because ye are not of the world, by I have chosen you out of the world, therefore the world hateth you," (John 15:18-19).

5. Lastly, this doctrine of election should fill the hearts of the godly with unspeakable rejoicing. Everlasting joy should be on their heads, and sorrow and mourning should fly away.

And, rather, they should consider the marvelous privileges of their election, and the wonderful happiness to which they are chosen of God. And you should do this if by the former signs you know yourself to be one of God's elect, consider the following:

1. First, you are sure of your salvation, and the glory of heaven when you die, "Whereunto he called you by the Gospel to obtain the glory of our Lord Jesus Christ," (2 Thessalonians 2:13-14).

2. The love of God to you is unchangeable, God will never cast off the people whom he has chosen, "God hath not cast away his people whom he knew before," (Romans 11:2).

3. You are sure of gracious entertainment in God's house, and sweet communion with God whilst you live, "Blessed is he whom thou choosest, and causest to come to thee: he shall dwell in thy courts, and we shall be satisfied with the pleasures of thine house, even of thine holy temple," (Psalm 65:4). "Therefore thus saith the Lord God, behold my servants shall eat, and ye shall be hungry: behold my servants shall drink, and ye shall be thirsty: behold my servants shall rejoice, and ye shall be ashamed. Behold my servants shall sing for joy of heart, and ye shall cry for sorrow of heart, and shall howl for vexation of mind," (Isaiah 65:13-14).

4. You shall be sure of protection against all adversaries that dare or rise up against you, "Fear thou not, for I am with thee: be not afraid, for I am thy God, I will strengthen thee, and will sustain thee with the right hand of my justice. Behold, all they that provoke thee shall be ashamed and confounded, they shall be as nothing; and they that strive with thee shall perish," (Isaiah 41:10-13).

5. Fifthly, all your afflictions shall be sweetened to you, and work together for the best, "Also we know that all things

work together for the good of them that love God, even to them that are called of his purpose," (Romans 8:28).

6. In all your suits to God, you are sure to have an audience, and compassionate respect, howsoever you are neglected in the world, "You have not chosen me, but I have chosen you, and ordained you, that ye go and bring forth fruit, and that your fruit remain, that whatsoever ye shall ask of the Father in my name, he may give it you," (John 15:16).

7. Christ will graciously communicate to you the secrets of God, and the mysteries of the kingdom, using you in it as a most dear and careful friend, (John 15:16, as stated before).

8. Lastly, all complaints brought to God against you, are sure to be nonsuited and cast out, so as nothing can be laid to your charge, nothing can condemn you, inasmuch as Christ has paid all your debts, and sits at the right hand of God to make requests for you, "Who shall lay anything to the charge of God's chosen: it is God that justifieth," (Romans 8:33).

CHAPTER 12:
Of Christ

"Neither is there salvation in any other: for among men there is given none other name under heaven, whereby we must be saved," (Acts 4:12).

We have considered election. The second fundamental means of grace is Christ, concerning whom the principles respect either:

1. His Person
2. His office

The principles concerning his person, look either,

1. On his divine nature
2. Or upon his human nature

The principle that concerns his divine nature is this: That Jesus Christ is very God; and that he is God, may be proved,

1. First, by testimony of Scripture, "For unto us a child is born, and unto us a son is given, and he shall call his name wonderful, counselor, the mighty God," (Isaiah 9:6). "In the beginning was the Word, and the Word was with God, and that Word was God," (John 1:1). "Of whom are the fathers, and of whom concerning the flesh, Christ came, who is God over all, blessed forever. Amen," (Romans 9:5). "And without controversy great is the mystery of godliness, which is, God is manifested in the flesh, justified in the Spirit," (1 Timothy 3:16). "But we know that the Son of God is come, and hath given us a mind to know him, which is true: and we are in him that is true, that is, in his Son Jesus Christ, this same is very God, and eternal life," (1 John 5:20).

2. By the divine properties given to him, as eternity, (John 1:1, 17:5); omnipotence, (John 3:31, Philippians 4:13). Savior, King of Kings, and the like.

3. By divine works done by him, as creation, (Colossians 1:16); forgiveness of sins, (Matthew 9:6); working of miracles, (John 10:25).

4. By the divine honor due unto him, as adoration, (Psalm 72:11; Hebrews 1:8) and believing in him.

5. By the conquest the Gospel has made in the world, (1 Timothy 3:16) and that not by any carnal power, (Zechariah 4:6).

6. By the patient suffering of his saints, "But they overcame him by the blood of the Lamb, and by the word of their testimony, and they loved not their lives unto the death," (Revelation 12:11).

Question. But why was it needful that he should be God?

Answer. for two causes chiefly.

1. The one was the greatness of our evil, which no creature could take off us, *viz.* 1. The grievousness of our sins; 2. The immense and intolerable weight of God's anger; 3. The empire of death; 4. The tyranny of the devil.

2. The other was the greatness of our good, which none but God could restore, *viz.* 1. An obedience to justify many; 2. The image of God, (1 Corinthians 1:30, Colossians 3:10).

If our Savior is the Son of God, yes, God himself, that holds in it no robbery to be equal with God. Then may it first serve for humiliation, and so,

1. To the world: in which this glorious light has risen, and yet their darkness comprehended it not, (John 1:5,10). To the very godly, because they are not so affected, as may become this marvelous glory of the Son of God; it should much abase

us, that we do not have thoughts and affections to take that notice we should of this Son of righteousness, so gloriously in the Gospel shining among us; we do not receive him, and conceive of him as this doctrine teaches us; how often has he come among his own, and his own did not receive him? (John 1:11).

2. For instruction, and so it should work in us,

1. Illumination, to see the greatness of the mystery of godliness that tells us of God manifested in the flesh, (1 Timothy 3:16). Our eyes should in this point receive sight and clearing. This doctrine should shine in our hearts, as the sun in the firmament; we should never rest informing ourselves in this, and praying for discerning, until after much neglect and unbelief past, we could say with Thomas, "My Lord and my God," (Matthew 16:16, John 20:28). This is the rock, on which the church is built.

2. The estimation of his sufferings for us; this blood of the New Testament, was the blood of God, (Acts 20:28).

3. The celebration of his praises is God over all; then let him be blessed forevermore, "Of whom are the fathers, and of whom concerning the flesh Christ came, who is God over all, blessed forever, Amen," (Romans 9:5).

4. The adoration of his person, when God brings forth his only begotten Son, let all the angels of heaven worship him, (Hebrews 1:4).

5. Faith: this should make us believe in him, and rely on the sufficiency of the redemption in him; yes, we should never rest, until we know him, and that we are in him. For this is eternal life, "The same came for a witness to bear witness of the light, that all men through him might believe," (John 1:7). "But we know that the Son of God is come, and hath given us a mind to know him, which is true, and we are in him that is true, that

is, in the Son Jesus Christ, the same is very God, and eternal life," (1 John 5:20).

3. The consideration of the divinity of Christ should wonderfully comfort us, and so it is used in diverse Scriptures. For if he is God, then he is full of grace to supply our needs, (John 1:14,16). He is infinite in righteousness to justify us, (Jeremiah 23:6). The government being on his shoulders. He will ever be known to be wonderful; as a Counselor to direct us, as a mighty God to defend us; as an everlasting Father to love us, and pity us, and spare us, and bare with our infirmities; as a Prince of peace, to preserve us in our reconciliation with God, and to fill us with peace that passes all understanding. And that we may not doubt of perseverance, the Prophet assures us that of the increase of his government and peace, there shall be no end; for he will order us, and establish us from now and forever.

CHAPTER 13:
Of Christ's Humanity

We have covered the divine nature of Christ. There are four principles concerning the human nature of Christ. The one concerns the matter, the other three concern the manner.

1. The first, that the Son of God was incarnate, assumed the true nature of man, and was a very man among us, "In the beginning was the Word, and the Word was with God, and that Word was God," (John 1:1). "And the Word was made flesh and dwelt among us, and we saw the glory thereof as the glory of the only begotten Son of the Father, full of grace and truth," (John 1:14). "Forasmuch then as the children were partakers of flesh and blood, he also himself likewise took part with them," (Hebrews 2:14). "For verily he took not on him the nature of angels; but he took on him the seed of Abraham," (Hebrews 2:16).

2. That he was not conceived as other men, but by the Holy Spirit, "And the angel answered and said unto her, the Holy Ghost shall come upon thee, and the power of the most high shall overshadow thee: therefore also that holy thing which shall be born of thee, shall be called the Son of God," (Luke 1:35). "Fear not to take Mary for thy wife; for that which is conceived in her is of the Holy Ghost," (Matthew 1:20).

3. That he was born of a virgin, "Therefore the Lord himself will give you a sign: behold the virgin shall conceive and bear a Son, and she shall call his name Emmanuel," (Isaiah 7:14). "Now the birth of Jesus Christ was thus: when as his mother Mary was betrothed to Joseph; before they came together she was found with child of the Holy Ghost," (Matthew 1:18). "I will also put enmity between thee and the woman, and

between thy seed and her seed, he shall break thine head, and thou shalt bruise his heel," (Genesis 3:15).

4. That his human nature subsisted in the divine nature, and so both made but one person, "For in him dwelleth all the fullness of the Godhead bodily," (Colossians 2:9). "And the angel answered and said unto her: The Holy Ghost shall come upon thee, and the power of the most high shall overshadow thee: therefore also that holy thing which shall be born of thee, shall be called the Son of God," (Luke 1:35).

The uses may be raised severally from each of the principles, and so, first, the doctrine of the incarnation of Christ may serve,

1. For information, and that both of the love of God, and of his wisdom, which both shine in this work. His love, in that he sent us a Savior to take our nature. And his wisdom, in that he sent his Son.

Question. But what need was there that Christ should be incarnate, and take man's nature rather than any other?

Answer: 1. First, that satisfaction might be made to God in the same nature that had offended.

2. Because without effusion of blood, there could be no remission, (Hebrews 9:22).

3. Because a Mediator should be meet to deal between both parties. Therefore, he is God for the business with his Father, and man for the business with men.

4. So that he might have the right of the kinsman to redeem us, and so of adoption, (Jeremiah 32:8; Ruth 3:13).

5. To assure our resurrection. "That he might destroy through death him that had the power of death, which is the devil," (Hebrews 2:14).

Question: but why was the second person in the Trinity incarnate?

Answer: It was most conveniently, and comely that it should be so?

1. By the Son the incarnation was planned at the beginning, and therefore fitly by him incarnate were sinners redeemed.

2. He most fitly repairs the image of God in us, who was himself the image of his Father.

3. He that was the Son of God most conveniently makes us the Sons of God.

2. Secondly, for instruction, and so it should teach us:

1. First, to acknowledge both natures in Christ, and know that it is of necessity to salvation to confess his glory in both.

2. It should work on us the impressions of humility. This is a matchless example of humility, that he that was equal to the Father, should make himself so low, as to take on him the form of a servant, as it is urged, (Philippians 2:6-7).

It would be an intolerable shame for us to mind our own things, or to stand on our glory, and greatness. O, how should this make us easily deny ourselves, if we could thoroughly think on it?

3. Thirdly, it should stir us up wonderfully to a desire to come to Christ, and to be made one with him, and to be like him. He drew near to us, when he took our nature; and shall not we draw near to him in imitation of his nature, and show forth his virtues? He descended from heaven to us, and shall we not ascend to heaven to him?

4. This may serve for great humiliation to all such as do not receive the Son of God: has he taken our nature, and dwelt amongst us, and we saw his glory, as the glory of the only begotten Son of God: and are we yet ignorant of him? Do we yet neglect to come to him?

5. Lastly, the incarnation of Christ is the very fountain of all our comfort. It is the sunshine of religion, we should rejoice in it above all things. There should be no godly man, but his heart should leap within him on the thoughts of this glorious grace of God. The angels of heaven sang in the air, when they brought this tiding; and can we fit any desolation in our heart, to whom a Savior is born, and for whom he was incarnate? (Luke 2:10).

Christ's incarnation is the most clear looking glass to show forth the wisdom, mercy, truth, and justice of God. This was a work far above the creation of man; this doctrine is comfortable in the very respect of the honor done to the nature of man, in that God has joined man so nearly to himself, and it imports a wonderful love, that Christ now unchangeably bears to man, being himself of the same nature. But especially it should swallow up all earthly discontentments to consider that God has given him to us, and Christ is all this for our sakes, "For unto us a child is born, and unto us a Son is given," (Isaiah 9:6). How should only Christ be something to us instead of all things? The very peace we have by him should inflame us, peace that is far above us, which resides with God and the angels. Peace within us with our own consciences; and peace about us with all creatures, (Luke 2:14); and specially it should establish us in the assurance of the accomplishment of all that yet remains of our full redemption, we need not doubt of his intercession. Our suits must all necessarily speed well, for there sits one at the right hand of God, that is our own flesh and blood, and we need not fear the last judgment. It cannot but be well with us, if our own brother is our Judge. We should not be afraid in the meantime in the evil day. He will succor us, he has had experience of the frailty of our nature, and therefore has a feeling of our infirmities, and will help us all in time of our need,

"For in that he suffered, and was tempted, he is able to succor them that are tempted," (Hebrews 2:18). "For we have not an high Priest, which cannot be touched with the feeling of our infirmities: but was in all things tempted in like sort, yet without sin," (Hebrews 4:15).

Yes, the very glory of Christ in heaven is by this means ours. Christ is my portion, my flesh, and my blood, where my portion reigns, there I believe that I reign; where my flesh is glorified, there I think myself in glory; where my blood rules, there I think myself exalted.

And all this is more comfortable if we consider that God had no respect of persons in this, which may appear by the manifestation of the incarnation. It was revealed to shepherds, and to the wise men; the one poor, the other rich; the one learned, the other unlearned; the one Gentiles, the other Jews; the one near, the other far off. This light appeared to Anna, a woman, as well as to Simeon, that just man. And besides, note the wonderful wisdom of God in the manner of revealing Christ; *viz.* to everyone according to his own estate. For to Simeon and Anna, as more spiritual persons, the nativity was revealed by the instinct of the Spirit. It was revealed to the shepherds, as more ruder men, by the voice and speech of angels. To the priests and scribes that searched Scripture, by an oracle of the Scripture. To Herod a stranger, by the testimony of the wise men that were strangers. To the wise men, that were students of astrology, by the rising of a new star.

CHAPTER 14:
The Conception of Christ

We have considered the uses of the incarnation of Christ. The uses of his conception follow. The doctrine of his conception by the Holy Spirit may serve:

1. First, for information, and that in diverse things.

1. First, concerning the wonder of his birth, here is a new birth given to the world, never such a one before. He that is the only Son in heaven, is by this means the only man on earth to be admired. When God was to be made visible on earth, and to come to dwell among men, a heavenly temple is provided for him; the Holy Spirit builds him a temple in the womb of a virgin.

2. Concerning the freedom of Christ from original sin, we might ask, how could Christ be free from sin, seeing he came of Adam, whose nature was infected in all his posterity.

Answer. Now this is answered in this principle: for Christ came *of Adam*, but not *by Adam*, but by the Holy Spirit. The Holy Ghost miraculously formed Christ's body of the substance of the virgin, stopping the course of original sin, and sanctifying it. Sin comes into the world only by propagation.

3. Concerning the sufficiency of the sacrifice of Christ. It must necessarily be an admirable sacrifice that is in this way fitted from the womb.

4. Concerning the superstition of the papists about the virgin Mary: for they attribute the purity of Christ's nature to the holiness of the virgin, that she was without sin; where it is evident that it is to be attributed to the Holy Spirit.

5. Concerning the possibility for Christ to be born of a virgin, it is as easy for God to frame to Christ a body in the

womb of a virgin, as to make man's body at the first of the mire of the earth.

2. Secondly, for instruction, and so this conception by the Holy Spirit should teach us:

1. First, to be wise to sobriety in this mystery of the incarnation of Christ: a purer sense and a purer hearing is called for here. The overshadowing of the virgin shows that we must bring faith to believe the mystery without further inquiring in the wrong way.

2. To desire fervently the sanctifying of our natures, that we as his members might be conformed to him as our head, and so we are, if Christ is conceived in our hearts by the Holy Spirit, as he was conceived in the womb of the virgin, (Galatians 4:7).

For consolation, and so his conception is comfortable, especially in two things:

1. First, the holiness of his conception will justify us from the unholiness of our conception, and acquit us from the guilt and filth of original sin.

2. Secondly, it may comfort us in the expectation of our perfect holiness. He that was so careful to have his natural body fitted so exquisitely, will not neglect his mystical body the church, but will love it, and wash it, until it is without spot and wrinkle, and the rather because it is bone of his bone, and flesh of his flesh, (Ephesians 5:25-26). And in this way we see the use of the conception.

CHAPTER 15:
Of Christ as Born of a Virgin

Thirdly, in that our Savior was born of a virgin it may serve,

1. For information, and so,

1. Concerning the marvelous wisdom of God in the manner of our salvation. By a woman came sin and death into the world. And so here the seed of the woman breaks the serpent's head. The devil got to be the god of the world by beguiling a woman. Now see how the Lord has devised to destroy his dominion by one made of a woman. They were both virgins affianced to husbands, but not yet known of man.

Question: But might some say, this is beyond belief, that a virgin should bring forth a child, and yet remain a virgin, having never known a man, this seems to be incredible.

Solution: If it had been a thing, which had no resemblance in nature, yet it had been nothing to believe the power of the God of nature. But yet there is instance of things born in nature without generation. The bees have young, and yet do not know marriage. The eastern bird, the phoenix is born, and newborn successively, and yet without parents; and shall we hold it beyond belief for God to do this great work upon him, who would was yet to restore the world. Christ is like a flower, which has heaven for his father, and earth for his mother.

Question: But how can it become the greatness of the Son of God, to abase himself to lie in the womb of the virgin?

Solution: The sun in the firmament does not receive any infection from any place, nor can anything cast into its fire something that will affect it; much less can the Son of God be polluted by being born of a virgin.

2. Secondly, this may furnish us with an argument against transubstantiation. The Scripture teaches us to believe that Christ was made of a woman, (Galatians 4:4) but not a word is there that he should be made of a piece of bread.

2. Secondly, God has created this new thing in the world, that a woman should compass a man? Why then do we go about? Why do we lose our labor? Why do we not settle our hearts directly on this Jesus, who is assigned us in this way wonderfully of God to be our way, our light, and our life? This very doctrine was used long since to rebuke men's extreme distractions, and loss of time, and labor in the way to the kingdom of heaven, (Jeremiah 31:21).

Yes, this doctrine ought to be to us God's sign that he will deliver us certainly, and fulfill all his promises; and it extremely threatens the unbelief of man, as the Prophet Isaiah urges it in the days of Ahaz, (Isaiah 7:14).

3. Thirdly, this should kindle in us a vehement desire to have God reveal his Son in us, and to have Christ born in our hearts: we think the virgin is blessed above women, that Christ was conceived in her womb; why certainly it is a great wonder, and *we* are blessed among men and women, if the Lord Jesus is conceived in our hearts, and we keep ourselves chaste virgins to him.

There have been four ways of making man:

1. The one was to make man without either man or woman; so was Adam made.

2. The second was to make man without a woman, so was Eve made.

3. The third was to make man both by man and woman, and so we their posterity are made.

4. The fourth way, was to make man without man by the woman only, and so was Christ made.

Now if we admire the first, second, and fourth of these; why should we not also admire the creating of a man, without womb, even in the heart of a man? Is it not a great wonder, that the Son of God should be formed in our breast; and yet such is the work of God in the new birth of a Christian. Christ is formed in them, "My little children, of whom I travail in birth again, until Christ be formed in you," (Galatians 4:9).

CHAPTER 16:
Of the Personal Union

And so we have considered the birth of Christ of a virgin. The personal union may serve both for information, and for consolation.

1. For information, concerning the marvelous glory of Christ, especially of the exaltation of the human nature. Here is a union singularly wonderful and wonderfully singular. No, what should I say, a union? Why? There are so many unions in Christ, that worthily all may be said to be gathered together in one in him. There is a natural, personal, mystical, and sacramental union in Christ.

The natural union is with the Father and the Holy Spirit, in one nature or essence. The personal union is this of the divine nature with the human in one person.

The mystical union is of Christ with the Church, in one body.

The sacramental union is of the body and blood of Christ with bread and wine in one ordinance. This union is not a union of inhabitation, as God dwells in the saints, nor only of consent, as the faithful are one in the Father and the Son, nor of co-mixing, as water and wine are one. It is also not of composition, when of two things is made some third thing in one. But I say it is a personal union, the human nature of Christ being assumed into union with the person of the Son of God. From where arises:

1. A special manner of subsisting in the human nature of Christ, differing from the other men. For soul and body make a person in other men, but not so in Christ. For his soul and body are born up and subsist in his divine nature. As the mistletoe

grows without a root of its own on the body of another tree, so is it with the human nature of Christ. As soul and body in us make one man, so God and man make one Christ in him.

2. A communication of properties; so as that which is proper to one nature, is attributed to the whole person. So the Son of God was crucified, and bought the church with his blood, (1 Corinthians 2:8; Acts 20:28).

3. The collation of gifts on the human nature after an unspeakable manner. In respect of which the human nature of Christ excels all creatures for wisdom, goodness, holiness, power, majesty, and glory, inasmuch as the Godhead dwells in him bodily, "For in him dwelleth all the fulness of the Godhead bodily," (Colossians 2:9); and so the second Adam far excels the first.

It was needful that Christ should be God and man in one nature.

1. So that he might reconcile or make God and man be one again.

2. So that he might be a fit Master, as being akin to both parties.

3. That he might pacify God by his death, which he could neither feel as God, nor overcome as man.

4. That the works of redemption done in the flesh might be a sufficient price for sin, by which the infinite God was wronged.

Here is also consolation in this doctrine: for from here arises a manifest reason of hope of pardon, and peace with God; and besides, out of all his fulness we may now all receive grace, and a supply for all our wants. Here we have all the treasures of wisdom and grace in the Christ-man; and he is now able to be a fountain of more good to us, than ever the first Adam was of evil.

CHAPTER 17:
Of Christ as Mediator

We have considered the principles concerning the person of Christ. His office follows. The principles concerning his office, consider it either in whole, or in parts.

1. The whole office of Christ is to be *a Mediator*, and so the principles that concern Christ's work of Mediator are five:

1. First, that there is but one Mediator between God and man, even Christ Jesus. "For there is one God, and one Mediator between God and man, which is the man Christ Jesus," (1 Timothy 2:5). "Neither is there salvation in any other: for amongst men there is given none other name under heaven whereby we must be saved," (Acts 4:12). "That is, that unto you is born this day in the city of David, a Savior, which is Christ the Lord," (Luke 2:11). Because there is none more merciful, (Hebrews 2:17), nor more able, (Hebrews 7:25).

2. That the cause of our salvation in his mediation is not merit in man, but grace in God and Christ, "Who hath saved us, and called us with an holy calling, not according to our works, but according to his own purpose and grace, which was given to us through Christ Jesus before the world was," (2 Timothy 1:9). "But when the bountifulness and love of God our Savior toward man appeared. Not by works of righteousness, which we had done, but according to his mercy he saved us by the washing of the new birth, and the renewing of the Holy Ghost," (Titus 3:4-5). "For by grace are ye saved through faith, and that not of yourselves; it is the gift of God," (Ephesians 2:8).

3. That this mediation was from the beginning of the world, and shall be to the end, "Jesus Christ yesterday, and today, the same also is forever," (Hebrews 13:8). "Which was

ordained before the foundation of the world, but was declared in the last times for your sakes," (1 Peter 1:20). "Therefore all that dwell upon the earth, shall worship him, whose names are not written in the book of life of the Lamb, which was slain from the beginning of the world," (Revelation 13:8).

For in the knowledge, destination, and acceptation of God, the two natures were accounted as united, and with him the things done, and to be done, present and to come; and all of these are considered together as one.

For explication of this principle, if we ask when the Mediator was given, it must be answered in three ways:

1. If we respect God's decree, he was given before all eternity, "As he hath chosen us in him before the foundation of the world," (Ephesians 1:4).

2. If we respect the virtue and efficacy of his mediation, he was given when need was from the beginning of the world, "Which was slain from the beginning of the world," (Revelation 13:8).

3. If we respect his manifestation in the flesh, he was given in the fulness of time: [2000] years ago, "But when thy fulness of time was come, God sent forth his Son made of a woman, and made under the law," (Galatians 4:4). "Who gave himself a ransom for all men, to be a testimony in due time," (1 Timothy 2:6).

4. That without the mediation of Christ no flesh can be saved, "Neither is there salvation in any other: for among men there is given none other name under heaven, whereby we must be saved," (Acts 4:12). "And enter not into judgment with thy servant, for in thy sight shall none that liveth be justified," (Psalm 143:2). "For in many things we sin all," (James 3:2).

5. That by the Mediator a new agreement or contract was made with God, "But this shall be the covenant that I will

make with the house of Israel: after those days saith the Lord, I will put my law in the inward parts, and write it in their hearts, and will be their God, and they shall be my people," (Jeremiah 31:33). "In that he saith a new Testament, he hath abrogated the old; now that which is disannulled and waxed old, is ready to vanish away," (Hebrews 8:13). "For there is no difference, for all have sinned, and fall short of the glory of God, and are justified freely by his grace through the redemption that is in Christ Jesus," (Romans 3:23-24). "Is the law then against the promise of God? God forbid: for if there had been a law given, which could have given life, surely righteousness should have been by the law. But the Scripture hath concluded all under sin, that the promise by the faith of Jesus Christ should be given to them that believe," (Galatians 3:21-22).

For the explication of this principle we must understand:

1. First, that the Scriptures make mention of three covenants, that God has made.

The one general, and earthly with all creatures about their preservation from the universal deluge, (Genesis 9), but of this covenant we have nothing else to consider here.

2. The second was the covenant called the *covenant of works*, this was made with all mankind in paradise, and stands still in force, since the fall, as men are in the estate of nature, the condition of which on man's part is in the moral law.

3. The third agreement made with man by means of the Mediator, called from the time of the fall to the days of Abraham, *the promise*, as being contrived in those words of promise, "I will also put enmity between thee and the woman, and between thy seed and her seed: He shall break thine head, and thou shalt bruise his heel," (Genesis 3:15).

From Abraham to Moses, it was called *the covenant,* (Genesis 17). From Moses to Christ, and so still *the Testament;* and as it stands in difference from the *covenant of works,* it may be called for all this time, *the covenant of grace.*

2. Secondly, that in this agreement with God by the Mediator, the mediator undertook for two things:

1. To pay all our debts, and satisfy God's justice, by a price of infinite value, "But he was wounded for our transgressions, he was broken for our iniquities, the chastisement of our peace was upon him, and with his stripes we are healed. All we like sheep have gone astray, we have turned everyone to his own way, and the Lord hath laid upon him the iniquity of us all," (Isaiah 53:5-6). "Then will he have mercy upon him, and will say deliver him, that he go not down into the pit: For I have received a reconciliation," (Job 33:24). "Who gave himself a ransom for all men to be a testimony in due time," (1 Timothy 2:6).

2. To purchase and merit for us God's favor and kingdom by a most absolute and perfect obedience, "To the praise of the glory of his grace, wherewith he hath made us accepted in his beloved," (Ephesians 1:6).

3. Thirdly, we must understand in what ways these new covenants agree, and in what ways they disagree.

These covenants agree in these two things: First, that they both were tendered to us by God. Secondly, that they both require a full and perfect righteousness, as the condition of eternal life. They differ:

1. In the manner of knowing them. For the *law* or *covenant of works* is known in some measure by nature, "Which shew the effect of the law written in their hearts, their conscience also bearing witness, and their thoughts accusing one another, or excusing," (Romans 2:15). But the Gospel or

covenant of grace is not known at all by nature. It is a mystery, "Which is the mystery hid, since the world began, and from all ages, but now is made manifest to his saints," (Colossians 1:26). "But we speak the wisdom of God in a mystery, even the hidden wisdom which God had determined before the world, unto our glory," (1 Corinthians 2:7). "But it is now made manifest by the appearing of our Savior Jesus Christ," (2 Timothy 1:10).

2. In the ministers of both, Moses was the minister of the law, but Christ of the Gospel, "For the law was given by Moses, but grace and truth came by Jesus Christ," (John 1:17).

3. In the means of attaining to the end common to both: the law is a law of works, and requires doing, or else it will not give wages. But the Gospel is a law of faith, requiring believing in him, that justifies the wicked, "But now is the righteousness of God made manifest without the law, having witness of the law, and of the prophets," (Romans 3:21). "But to him that worketh not, but believeth in him that justifieth the ungodly, his faith is counted for righteousness," (Romans 4:5). "For Moses thus describeth the righteousness which is of the law: that the man which doth these things shall live thereby," (Romans 10:5).

Again, the law requires perfect righteousness in our own persons, but the Gospel offers the righteousness of another to be received by faith, "For what the law could not do, in that it was weak through the flesh, God sending his own Son in the likeness of sinful flesh, and for sin, condemned sin in the flesh: That the righteousness of the law might be fulfilled in us, who walk not after the flesh, but after the Spirit," (Rom. 8:3-4). "For as by one man's disobedience many were made sinners; so by the obedience of one shall many also be made righteous," (Romans 5:19). "For Christ is the end of the law for righteousness, unto everyone that believeth," (Romans 10:4).

The law requires our debts, every farthing, the Gospel publishes the acquittance of the principal, by reason of the satisfaction of the surety. The law gives heaven, as wages for work done; the Gospel gives heaven *gratis.*

4. In effects or efficacy; the law requires good works, but gives no power to do them, "Yet the Lord hath not given you an heart to perceive, and eyes to see, and ears to hear unto this day," (Deuteronomy 29:4). But the Gospel gives the Spirit of God, which works what he requires, "But this shall be the covenant that I will make with the house of Israel: After those days, saith the Lord, I will put my law in their inward parts, and write it in their hearts, and will be their God, and they shall be my people," (Jeremiah 31:33). "And I will put my Spirit within you, and cause you to walk in my statutes, and ye shall keep my judgments, and do them," (Ezekiel 36:27). "For if the ministry of condemnation was glorious, much more does the ministration of righteousness exceed in glory," (2 Corinthians 3:9).

The law shows the disease, and the Gospel cures it, "But now we are delivered from the law being dead unto it, wherein we were holden, that we should serve in newness of spirit, and not in the oldness of the letter," (Romans 7:6). "O wretched man that I am, who shall deliver me from the body of this death?" (Romans 7:24).

The knowledge of sin is by the law, but that which heals us is the tidings of remission in Jesus Christ.

5. In the persons, to whom they belong. The law is for the unrighteous, "Knowing this, that the law is not given unto a righteous man, but unto the lawless and disobedient, to the ungodly, and to the sinners, to the unholy, and to the profane," (1 Timothy 1:9).

But the Gospel belongs to the poor and penitent, "The Spirit of the Lord is upon me, because he hath anointed me, that I should preach the Gospel to the poor; he hath sent me, that I should heal the broken heart, that I should preach deliverance to the captives, and recovering of sight to the blind, that I should set at liberty them, that are bruised," (Luke 4:18).

The uses may be:

1. First, for consolation to all the godly, and this comfort in their Mediator, and the new covenant in him may be the more distinctly formed in us, if we consider,

1. The privileges and benefits we reap by this new covenant.

2. The properties of the covenant.

3. The persons to whom it may belong.

1. For the first, by means of the Mediator in this New Covenant, we receive many admirable prerogatives and blessings, as:

1. The abrogation of the old covenant, "In that he saith a New Testament, he hath abrogated the old: now that which is disannulled, and waxed old, is ready to vanish away," (Hebrews 8:13). So as now we are not under the law, but under grace, "For sin shall not have dominion over you: for ye are not under the law, but under grace," (Romans 6:14).

2. Communion of saints from all parts of the world: men of all nations coming in upon this new agreement, "And he said, it is a small thing, that thou shouldest be my servant, to raise up the tribes of Jacob, and to restore the desolations of Israel: I will also give thee for a light of the Gentiles, that thou mayest be my salvation unto the ends of the world," (Isaiah 49:6,11). "But I say unto you, that many shall come from the east and west, and shall sit down with Abraham, Isaac, and Jacob in the Kingdom of heaven," (Matthew 8:11).

3. Reconciliation with God, and the pardon of all sins, "For God was in Christ, and reconciled the world to himself, not imputing their sins unto them," (2 Corinthians 5:19). "But this shall be the covenant that I will make with the house of Israel, after those days, saith the Lord, I will be their God, and they shall be my people. And I will forgive their iniquity, and will remember their sins no more," (Jeremiah 31:33-34). "And for this cause is he the Mediator of the New Testament, that through death, which was for the redemption of the transgressions, that were in former testament," (Hebrews 9:15).

4. A righteousness answerable to that of the law wrought for us, and imputed to us, "That the righteousness of the law might be fulfilled in us, which walk not after the flesh, but after the Spirit," (Romans 8:4).

5. The inhabitation of the Spirit of God taking possession of us unto God's use forever, "And I will make this my covenant with them, saith the Lord; my Spirit that is upon thee, and my words which I have put in thy mouth, shall not depart out of thy mouth, nor out of the mouth of thy seeds seed, saith the Lord, even from henceforth forever," (Isaiah 59:21).

6. The law of God put into our hearts from the least to the greatest, "But this shall be the covenant that I will make with the house of Israel: After those days, saith the Lord, I will put my law in their inward parts, and write it in their hearts," (Jeremiah 31:33).

7. A covenant with all creatures, who must be at peace with us, and serviceable to us, "And in that day will I make a covenant for them with the wild beasts, and with the fowls of the heaven, and with that, that creepeth upon the earth: and I will break the bow, and the sword, and the battle out of the earth, and I will make them to sleep safely. And in that day I will hear, saith the Lord, I will even hear the heavens, and they

shall hear the earth. And the earth shall hear the corn, and the wine, and the oil, and they shall hear Israel," (Hosea 2:18,21-22).

8. God's sanctuary in the midst of us, and his presence with us forever, "Moreover, I will make a covenant with them of peace: it shall be an everlasting covenant with them, and will set my sanctuary amongst them forevermore. My tabernacle also shall be with them, yea I will be their God, and they shall be my people," (Ezekiel 37:26-28).

9. The promise of an eternal inheritance, "And for this cause is he the Mediator of the New Testament, that through death, which was for the redemption of the transgressions that were in the former testament, they which were called, might receive the promise of eternal inheritance," (Hebrews 9:15).

The second part of the consolation may be raised from the consideration of the properties of the covenant, which are:

1. That it is free, and God does not stand upon desert in us, "Lo, everyone that thirsteth, come ye to the waters; and ye that have no silver, come buy, and eat: come, I say, buy wine, and milk without silver, and without money. Wherefore do you lay out silver, and not for bread? And your labor without being satisfied? Hearken diligently unto me, and eat that which is good, and let your soul delight in fatness. Behold, I gave him for a witness to the people, for a Prince and a Master unto the people," (Isaiah 55:1-2,4).

2. That it is unchangeable and eternal, "For the mountains shall remove, and the hills shall fall down; but my mercy shall not depart from thee, neither shall the covenant of my peace fall away, saith the Lord, that hath compassion on thee," (Isaiah 54:10).

And we may the rather be assured of this, if we consider:

1. The nature of God: Mercy pleases him, and he is so desirous of reconciliation, that he implores men to be reconciled, (2 Corinthians 5:19-20; Hosea 2:19).

2. The propitiation in Christ God has proclaimed it from heaven, that in him he is well pleased, and fully pacified, (Matthew 3:17). And Christ is given for a covenant of the people, (Isaiah 49:8).

3. That there is an act for it in the counsel of God from everlasting, (1 Corinthians 2:7).

4. That God has sworn to keep this covenant, (Hebrews 6:18, 7:19-22; Isaiah 42:6-7).

5. That it is confirmed by the death of the testator, (Hebrews 9:16, Matthew 26:27).

6. Because he ever lives to make request for us at the right hand of God, and is able perfectly to save those that come unto him, (Hebrews 7:25, 13:8).

7. Because the law cannot disannul it, (Galatians 3:17).

8. That we have sacraments to confirm it, and seal it. And if we can be persuaded that the flood shall come no more, when we see the rainbow; how much more should the glorious sacraments of the new covenant, settle us in the assurance of the unchangeableness of God's good will towards us?

9. That the covenant is kept, not only in the word, which cannot be blotted out, but also, we have the keeping of it in our own hearts, (Romans 10:4-5).

10. That God is now long since known to be in the church by the name of Jehovah, which notes both his constancy and all-sufficiency, (Exodus 6:3).

3. This is comfortable if we consider the persons that may be capable of the privileges of this New Covenant. God does not stand upon desert, (Isaiah 55:1) the stranger and the eunuchs may be as well accepted here as the sons and

daughters, if their hearts are sincere with God, (Isaiah 56:4,6) the abject Gentiles are not excluded, (Isaiah 49:7).

What should I say, the whole world is invited, and worlds of people may be reconciled to God, (2 Corinthians 5:19).

And as this is comfortable at all times, so there is comfort to be gathered out of it in special distresses, as

1. In the case of sin.

2. In the case of affliction.

3. In the case of death.

1. For the first, in the case of sin after calling, it is a memorable place, "My babes these things write I unto you, that ye sin not: and if any man sin, we have an advocate with the Father, Jesus Christ the righteous," (1 John 2:1).

2. For the second: in the case of affliction, there are many Scriptures that have recourse to this doctrine of comfort. If the godly are grieved and oppressed, and come to God, and humble themselves, the Lord will remember this covenant, and hear them, as Exodus 2:2,4-5, Exodus 6:4-6, and Leviticus 26:41-42.

The godly know in all afflictions, whom they have trusted, and ought to believe, that he will yet keep, which by covenant is committed to him, (2 Timothy 1:12). Christ has commissioned from God by virtue of this covenant to say to the prisoners, go forth, and to them that are in darkness, show yourselves, (Isaiah 49:9-10). For a small moment God may forsake, but with great mercy will he gather us. In a little wrath I hid my face from thee for a moment, but with everlasting kindness will I have mercy on thee saith the Lord thy redeemer. For this is as the waters of Noah. The mountains may depart but his kindness, and the covenant of his peace shall not depart, nor be removed, the Lord says, that has mercy on us, (Isaiah 54:7-11).

3. For the third, in the case of death, it is a known instance of Job, how he comforted himself in his Redeemer, in the midst of all his wonderful distresses, that seemed to threaten his death (as it were) every moment, "For I know that my redeemer liveth, and that he shall stand at the latter day upon the earth," (Job 19:25).

In this way of the uses for consolation. The instructions follow, and may be cast into two sorts. For this doctrine of the new covenant in the Mediator may teach us; 1. Both what to avoid; 2. And what to do.

1. The conceit of merit of our own works, and all boasting of any worthiness in ourselves. For this were to make the promise of none effect, and the grace of this new covenant void. It would be to stand in the old covenant, "For if they which are of the law be heirs, faith is made void, and the promise is made of none effect," (Romans 4:14). "Where is then thy rejoicing? It is excluded: by what law? of works: nay, but by the law of faith," (Romans 3:27). "For Christ is the end of the law for righteousness unto everyone that believeth," (Romans 10:4).

2. The forgetfulness of God; whatsoever befalls us, we should not forget God, nor deal wickedly in his covenant, "All this is come upon us, yet do we not forget thee, neither deal we falsely concerning thy covenant," (Psalm 44:17).

The duties we should do, may be referred to two sorts: for either, 1. They are such as fit us for this new covenant; 2. Or such as we should do to walk worthy of it. If we would have any comfort by the Mediator, and this new agreement with God,

1. We must turn from our transgressions, else we have no redeemer, "And the Redeemer shall come unto Zion, and unto them that turn from iniquities in Jacob, saith the Lord," (Isaiah 59:20). We must be new creatures, all things in us must now be new, our old things must be passed and given over, (2 Corinthians 5:17-19). Going and weeping we should go, and ask for the way, (Jeremiah 50:4).

2. Secondly, we must come to Christ being weary, and laden, and receive him, and lay hold upon him by faith. This new agreement is chiefly published for the obedience of faith, (Romans 16:26, Romans 3:25).

That we may walk worthy of this covenant, we must look to diverse things,

1. First, we should inflame our hearts to the love of the Lord Jesus, and be ready to acknowledge his wonderful love to us, that dedicated this testament with his blood, (Hebrews 9:16, Isaiah 59:16).

2. God should be our portion forever, "My flesh faileth, and my heart also: but God is the strength of my heart, and my portion forever," (Psalm 73:26). What now should be our hope? Our hope should even be in God, "And now Lord what wait I for, my hope is even in thee?" (Psalm 39:7). We should for all other things of this life confess ourselves to be strangers, and pilgrims, and embrace only these new promises of a better happiness, (Hebrews 11:13).

3. We should never be ashamed of the testimony of the Lord, nor of this doctrine of the Mediator, for all the papists in the world who would dissuade us from the Gospel; but partake willingly of all the afflictions that may befall us for this glad tidings in the Gospel, (2 Timothy 1:8-13). But rather glory in our singular riches, which is Christ in us, (Colossians 1:27).

4. We should strive to live like such as are now again confederates of God, and as may become the singular prerogatives of our new estate. This is briefly comprehended in those few words, "Walk before God and be upright," (Genesis 17:1, Isaiah 59:17-19).

5. We should be in a special manner careful, that the salt of the covenant of God is not lacking, (Leviticus 2:13). This is the salt of discretion, and of mortification. God's confederates should be a wise and humble people, (Mark 9:50).

6. If ever we fall into distress, we must run to God, and urge him with his covenant, and deprecate his displeasure, "Do not abhor us for thy namesake, cast not down the throne of thy glory. Remember and break not thy covenant with us," (Jeremiah 14:21).

7. We should forever cleave unto God with full purpose of heart in a perpetual covenant never to be forgotten, (Jeremiah 50:5).

8. We should learn of God how to carry ourselves in all agreements and covenants with men.

We should be easy to be reconciled, and keep our promises, though made with disadvantage. Ministers also may learn from these principles, how to divide the word. The law is to be preached to the unrighteous, and this new covenant of promise in Christ to the penitent and humble soul, (1 Timothy 1:9, Luke 4:18).

The last use may be for terror unto all wicked men that live in the Church, and securely sin on without regard of reconciliation, or seeking the benefits of this new covenant. Who can express their misery, which receives aggravation from their neglect of this grace offered, these are children of the bondwoman, (Galatians 4:24). Upon these God will fearfully avenge the quarrel of his covenant, (Leviticus 26:25, Isaiah 24:5,

Jeremiah 34:18, Ezekiel 20:36-37). Though they cry to God, he will not know them, (Hosea 8:1-3). Their covenant with death and hell shall be dissolved, (Isaiah 28:15). For they are all under the curse, (Galatians 3:10). Yes, if the Lord proceeds to take his guidance and beauty, and cut it asunder, and dissolve even his public covenant he has made with the nations, O how then beyond all hope of cure would be their miserable condition! Or if he does not do that, yet if he removes their candlestick, by taking the means from them, how will these people (whole congregations that forget God) be turned into hell, and all their multitudes!

CHAPTER 18:
Of the Prophetic Office of Christ

We have considered the principles that look on the office of Christ completely. The principles that concern the parts of his office follow.

First, there are three sorts or parts of the offices of Christ:

1. His prophetic office.

2. His priestly office.

3. His regal or kingly office.

This division may be proved by two ways:

1. By the degrees of man's misery: there are three degrees of man's misery:

1. Ignorance of the evil into which he is plunged, and of the good he lacks.

2. *Ataxia* or a disorder in all parts of his heart and life.

3. Guiltiness arising by this:

Now in the offices of Christ is a threefold remedy.

1. His prophecy heals ignorance.

2. His kingdom takes away disorder.

3. His priesthood abolishes guiltiness.

2. By the parts of the typical anointing in the Old Testament. For by oil there was a threefold inauguration: 1. Of prophets; 2. Of priests; 3. Of kings, which shadowed out by external oil the anointing of Christ.

1. First, of the prophetic office of Christ:

1. What it is.

2. Its parts.

3. The manner of executing it.

1. The prophecy or prophetic offices of Christ is his work by which he instructs his church concerning the will of God, especially his secret counsel about redeeming mankind.

2. The parts are two: first, the external promulgation of doctrine. Secondly, the internal illumination of the heart, or the making of the doctrine effectual by the Spirit, renewing and inclining the mind and will of man.

The external promulgation of doctrine has three things in it:

1. The preaching of the Gospel, or the doctrine concerning God's grace or redemption in Christ, (Isaiah 61:1).

2. The interpretation of the law according to the mind of the lawgiver.

3. Prediction of things to come.

3. The manner of execution of this office was:

1. Mediately by patriarchs and prophets in the Old Testament: and by Apostles and ministers of the Gospel in the New Testament.

2. Immediately, and that either by his divine nature, or both natures: By his divine nature he instructed the patriarchs and prophets in the Old Testament by visions, oracles, and dreams. By both natures, by word of mouth in the New Testament he himself taught amongst men, (1 Peter 3:19, 1 John 1:5).

The principles concerning the prophetic office of Christ are:

1. That in Christ are all the treasures of wisdom and knowledge, "In whom are hid all the treasures of wisdom and knowledge," (Colossians 2:3).

2. That it is only Christ, that reveals the truth out of the bosom of his Father, "All things are given unto me of my Father, and no man knoweth the Son but the Father: neither knoweth

any man the Father but the Son, and he to whom the Son will reveal him," (Matthew 11:27). "No man hath seen God at any time, the only begotten Son which is in the bosom of the Father, he hath revealed him," (John 1:18). "Then Simon Peter answered him, Master, to whom shall we go, thou hast the words of eternal life," (John 6:68).

3. That Christ has himself taught doctrine among men, "In these last days he has spoken unto us by his Son," (Hebrews 1:2). "The Spirit of the Lord God is upon me, therefore hath the Lord anointed me; he hath sent me to preach good tidings unto the poor, to bind up the brokenhearted, to preach liberty to the captives, and to them that are bound, the opening of the prison," (Isaiah 61:1).

4. That he has revealed the whole counsel of God, "For all things that I have heard of my Father, have I made known unto you," (John 15:15). "For I have given unto them the words which thou gavest me, and they have received them, and have known surely that I came out from thee," (John 17:8). "I will raise them up a Prophet from among their brethren like unto thee; and will put my words into his mouth, and he shall speak unto them all that I shall command him," (Deuteronomy 18:18).

5. That the ministry in the church is by authority from Christ, "Wherefore behold, I send unto you the prophets, and wise men, and scribes," (Matthew 22:34). "He therefore gave some to be Apostles, and some Prophets, and some Evangelists, and some Pastors and Teachers. Now then are we ambassadors for Christ, as though God did beseech ye through us, we pray you in Christ's stead, that ye be reconciled to God," (2 Corinthians 5:20).

6. That the whole efficacy of doctrine either recorded in Scriptures, or from there taught unto men, depends upon Christ, "Knowing this first, that no prophecy of the scripture is

of any private interpretation. For the prophecy came not in old time by the will of man: but holy men of God spake as they were moved by the Holy Ghost," (2 Peter 1:20-21). "I have planted, Apollos watered, but God gave the increase," (1 Corinthians 3:6).

7. That the prophecy of Christ belongs generally to all nations, "And he said, it is a small thing, that thou shouldst be my servant to raise up the tribes of Jacob, and to restore the desolations of Israel. I will also give thee for a light of the Gentiles, that thou mayest be my salvation unto the end of the world," (Isaiah 49:6); though especially Christ was sent unto the lost sheep of Israel, "But he answered, and said, I am not sent but unto the lost sheep of Israel," (Matthew 15:24). "He shall speak peace unto the heathen, and his dominion shall be from sea unto sea, and from the river unto the end of the land," (Zechariah 9:10).

These principles may serve:

1. For information, and that of diverse things:

1. First, we may by this understand the reason why Christ is called the messenger, the Angel of the covenant, the Word, Wisdom; the Minister of circumcision; Pastor, Doctor, Archbishop; the Apostle of our profession, and namely, because of his prophetship, and ministry in revealing God's will to the church.

2. We may here take notice of the dignity of the ministry; we all serve under Christ, and have our commissions signed, and sealed by him. Christ himself was a minister of circumcision, (Romans 15:8). And anointed to preach the Gospel, (Isaiah 61:1).

And he works mighty things by the service of men, and that the calling might be the more honorable, he would not write Scripture himself, nor continue his preaching, but left both to his servants (so the head dictated and the members wrote it). Wherefore let men esteem us as the dispensers of the secrets of Christ, (1 Corinthians 4:1-2) and be persuaded by us, (2 Corinthians 5:20).

3. Thirdly, we must here know that we must depend upon Christ only for doctrine needful to salvation. There is but one Lawgiver: away with traditions and revelations of men's own hearts; if an angel from heaven would teach us otherwise, let him be accursed, (Galatians 1:8; James 4:12). Will any man teach God? (Job 21:22).

4. We may here see the horrible estate of such as will be still ignorant and live in their sins, having the Scriptures and preaching in the name, and by the authority of Christ, (John 1:10, 3:19). Christ in these cries to them, but men do not regard, (Proverbs 1:20).

5. We must take heed that we do not make a mistake, and that in two things.

1. First, about the difference of Christ, and all others in teaching.

2. About the continuance of this prophetic office: Christ's teaching in his own person excelled all others, so as we might truly say, who teaches like him? (Job 36:22).

1. For first he taught with more authority, "For he taught them, as one having authority, and not as the scribes," (Matthew 7:29).

2. He teaches by his Spirit, not by sound of words only, or by ink and paper.

3. He engraves his words not in stone, but in the fleshly tables of men's hearts, (2 Corinthians 3:3). And for the continuance of prophecy, we must know that it lasts but for this life: for in the other world prophecy shall cease, "Love doth never fall away, though that prophesyings be abolished, or the

tongues cease, or knowledge vanisheth away," (1 Corinthians 13:8).

2. For instruction, and so these principles may teach,

1. First, all in general, and so diverse duties:

1. First, with all carefulness therefore to hear the voice of Christ, "Behold, there came a voice out of the cloud, saying, This is my beloved Son, in whom I am well pleased; hear him," (Matthew 17:5).

2. In all this it requires us to run to Christ, and pray that he would teach us, "Lead me forth in thy truth, and teach me: for thou art the God of my salvation: In thee do I trust all the day," (Psalm 25:5). "Teach me to do thy will, for thou art my God, let thy good Spirit lead me into the land of righteousness," (Psalm 143:10).

3. But then, if we would ever profit by Christ's teaching, we must be poor in spirit, broken in heart, and mourn for our sins, (Isaiah 60:1; Malachi 3:1-7). And make a conscience effort to leave all sin, and be removed throughout, (Ephesians 4:17-23).

4. To love the house of God, where the Son of God exercises his prophesying, "Blessed are they that dwell in thine house, they will ever praise thee: For a day in thy courts is better than a thousand otherwhere; I had rather be a doorkeeper in the house of my God, than to dwell in the tabernacles of wickedness," (Psalm 84:4, 10). We should long for it, and call upon one another, (Isaiah 2:3).

5. To cleave to the counsels, reproofs, doctrines, and exhortations of Christ in the execution of his office, (John 6:68). And to receive the truth with all full assurance, (Hebrews 3:6; 2 Peter 1:19).

6. Not to be too busy one against another in doubtful or indifferent things, "There is one Lawgiver, which is able to save

and destroy; who art thou that judgest another man?" (James 4:11-12).

2. Secondly, here ministers may learn diverse things:

1. Not to affect the praise of men for the greatness of their gifts, or glory of their work. They must not be called Rabbi, seeing they have a Doctor, even Christ, and they have nothing, but what they have received from him, (Matthew 23:8). But rather learn of John the Baptist, (John 3:30-31) who said, "He must increase, but I must decrease.

2. When they discharge their duties; not to be afraid of men, or to be overmuch careful in their trouble, what to speak or do. They should settle this in their hearts; for Christ will give them a mouth and wisdom, which all their adversaries shall not be able to gainsay, or resist; one hair of their head shall not perish, and therefore in patience they should possess their souls, (Luke 21:14-20).

3. To be diligent in the execution of their office, seeing they must make up their accounts to Christ, whose ambassadors they are, and they should speak as the words of Christ, and not their own words, (Romans 12:6-8).

3. Thirdly, here is singular consolation to all the godly from the prophetic office of Christ, and that if we consider three things:

1. What Christ will teach us.

2. How he will teach us.

3. Whom he will teach.

1. For the first, it may be an exceeding comfort that God has given us his Son to be our Prophet. For by this we may be assured that he will be our counselor in all estates, (Isaiah 9:6). He will teach us to profit, (Isaiah 33:22). And when we are dejected and broken in heart, and mourn for our corruptions, he acknowledges it to be a part of his office to apply the Gospel

to us, and to proclaim the acceptable year of the Lord, and to pour upon us the oil of gladness for the Spirit of heaviness.

2. For the second: Christ's teaching is wonderfully comfortable; for the Scripture shows that he will teach us,

1. Freely he will give us our teaching, he does not stand on being hired, "For I have given unto them the words, which thou gavest me," (John 17:8).

2. Powerfully and effectually, so as if our hearts were dead within us, yet he will revive them; the dead shall hear his voice, (John 5:25).

3. Familiarity, and with great delight, as a mother would instruct her child at home in a chamber, (Song of Solomon 8:2).

4. Fully: keeping from us nothing that may be needful for us, he will teach us all things, "Henceforth call I you not servants: for the servant knoweth not what his Master doth, but I have called you friends: for all things that I have heard of my Father, have I made known unto you?" (John 15:15). "In whom are hid all the treasures of wisdom, and knowledge," (Colossians 2:3).

5. Gloriously, and with a marvelous shining light of knowledge; that may ravish our hearts, and much affect us, "For God, that commanded the light to shine out of darkness, is he which hath shined in our hearts to give the light of the knowledge of the glory of God in the face of Jesus Christ," (2 Corinthians 4:6). "But we all behold as in a mirror, the glory of the Lord with open face, and are changed into the same image from glory to glory, as by the Spirit of the Lord," (2 Corinthians 3:18).

6. Confidently: He will so teach us the truth, as he will be ready to justify it, as a never failing faithful, and true witness, "And unto the angel of the Church of the Laodiceans write,

These things saith Amen the faithful, and the true witness, the beginning of the creatures of God," (Revelation 3:14). "Behold I gave him for a Witness to the people, for a Prince, and a Master unto the people," (Isaiah 55:4).

7. Inwardly, as well as outwardly: To this end he has given us the anointing, even his Spirit in our hearts to teach us all things, "But the anointing which ye received of him dwelleth in you, and ye need not that any man teach you: but as the same anointing teacheth you of all things, and it is true, and is not lying, and as it taught you, you shall abide in him.

8. Compassionately with singular tenderness, fitting himself to everyone's nature and ability, "I am the good Shepherd; the good Shepherd giveth his life for his sheep," (John 10:11). "And I will set up a Shepherd over them, and he shall feed them, even my servant David, he shall feed them, and he shall be their shepherd," (Ezekiel 34:23). "He shall feed his flock like a Shepherd, he shall gather the lambs with his arm, and carry them in his bosom, and shall guide them with young," (Isaiah 40:11).

3. For the third: It is exceedingly comfortable that he will teach all that come unto him, even all that are given to him of God, all the godly, of what sex, condition, or nation soever; "They shall all be taught of God, from the least to the greatest:" Simple things, as well as those of higher forms, "And all thy children shall be taught of the Lord, and much peace shall be to thy children," (Isaiah 54:13). "And they shall teach no more every man his neighbor, and every man his brother, saying, Know the Lord: for they shall all know me from the least of them to the greatest of them, saith the Lord," (Jeremiah 31:34).

And therefore, let us observe these things, and acknowledge this goodness, and receive his testimony: for by this we seal that God is true, "He that hath received his testimony, hath sealed, that God is true," (John 3:33). So much now considering his prophetic office.

CHAPTER 19:
Of the Priestly Office of Christ

The priestly office of Christ follows, which is that part of his function by which he makes satisfaction to God for men. This office in the execution of it has in it three things; or there are three things Christ must do, as the Priest of the church:

1. He must obey the law of God perfectly.

2. He must make expiation for our sins by sacrificing to God.

3. He must make intercession for us.

1. First, of the principles that concern his obedience; there are four things we are bound to believe concerning the obedience of Christ:

1. First, that he was without sin in his nature, "Which of you can rebuke me of sin?" (John 8:46). "For he hath made him to be sin for us, which knew no sin," (2 Corinthians 5:21). "But with the precious blood of Christ, as of a Lamb undefiled and without spot," (1 Peter 1:19). "Who did no sin, neither was their guile found in his mouth," (1 Peter 2:22-23). "For we have not an high Priest which cannot be touched with the feeling of our infirmities, but was in all things tempted in like sort, yet without sin," (Hebrews 4:15).

2. Secondly, that he fulfilled the whole law of God perfectly in all his actions. Here he is called the holy one, and the holy child Jesus, "Because thou wilt not leave my soul in hell, neither wilt suffer thine holy one to see corruption," (Acts 2:27). "But ye denied the holy one, and the just," (Acts 3:14). "So that thou stretch forth thine hand, that healing, and signs, and wonders may be done by the name of thine holy Son Jesus,"

(Acts 4:30). "But ye have an ointment from him that is holy, and ye have known all things," (1 John 2:20).

3. Thirdly, that he fulfilled the law, not only for himself as one who kept it perfectly, but for us, and for our sakes, "For (that that was impossible to the law, inasmuch as it was weak because of the flesh) God sending his own Son in the similitude of sinful flesh, and for sin condemned sin in the flesh. That the righteousness of the law might be fulfilled in us, which walk not after the flesh, but after the Spirit," (Romans 8:3-4). "For Christ is the end of the law, for righteousness unto everyone that believeth," (Romans 10:4). "Likewise then, as by the offense of one, the fault came on all men to condemnation; so by the justifying of one, the benefit abounded toward all men to the justification of life," (Romans 5:18).

4. That his righteousness is an everlasting righteousness, that is, such a righteousness as serves for the elect of all ages, and such a righteousness as cannot be lost, "Seventy weeks are determined upon thy people, and upon thine holy city to finish thy wickedness, and to seal up the sins, and to reconcile the iniquity, and to bring in everlasting righteousness," (Daniel 9:24).

The uses may be,

1. For consolation: For by this all the faithful may be assured that though they are very unrighteous in themselves, yet they are made the righteousness of God in him, "In his days Judah shall dwell safely; and this is the name whereby they shall call him, The Lord our righteousness," (Jeremiah 23:6). "For he hath made him to be sin for us, which knew no sin, that we should be made the righteousness of God in him," (2 Corinthians 5:21).

He is the end of the law to everyone that believes. We have a certain justification to life by his obedience, as ever we were subject to death by Adam's disobedience, "For as by one man's disobedience many were made sinners; so by the obedience of one shall many be made righteous," (Romans 5:19).

And if his righteousness is ours, how rich are we? And how ought our hearts to be established in his well doing?

2. Secondly, for instruction: and so it should work in us two things:

1. First, an establishment of faith in our reconciliation, and a willing yielding of ourselves to acknowledge this free gift of God in his Son, (2 Corinthians 5:21, Romans 10:4).

2. Secondly, an imitation of his marvelous holiness; a striving to express his virtues, that we may be holy as he is holy; for he communicates the benefit of his obedience only to such as live justly, and walk not after the flesh, but after the Spirit, "That the righteousness of the law might be fulfilled in us, which walk not after the flesh, but after the Spirit," (Romans 8:4). "But ye are a chosen generation, a royal priesthood, an holy nation, a peculiar people, that ye should shew forth the virtues of him, that hath called you out of darkness into his marvelous light," (1 Peter 2:9). "Take my yoke on you, and learn of me, that I am meek, and lowly in heart, and ye shall find rest unto your souls," (Matthew 11:29). "Therefore if any man be in Christ, let him be a new creature," (2 Corinthians 5:17).

3. Thirdly, for humiliation to all stubborn-hearted wicked men, that deny this holy one, partly by their unbelief, when they do not regard his words, whom they can convince of no sin, "Which of you can rebuke me of sin? And if I say the truth, why do you not believe me?" (John 8:47).

And partly by a wicked life keeping out all conformity with Christ; as also choosing rather to live in wicked company, than to cleave to Christ. Is this not to deny the holy one, and to choose a murderer to be given them, (Acts 3:14)? What communion is there between Christ and Belial? between his righteousness, and such unrighteousness? So much for considering his obedience to the law.

CHAPTER 20:
Of the Expiation of Sin

The principles that concern the expiation of sin follow. This expiation was made by the passion of Christ, concerning which we must believe these things of necessity:

1. That the passion of Christ was by the decree and everlasting fore-appointment of God, "Him, I say, have ye taken by the hands of the wicked, being delivered up by the determinate counsel and foreknowledge of God," (Acts 2:23).

2. That the sufferings of Christ were for our sins, and for our sakes, so as he bore all our iniquities, "Who his own self bare our sins in his body on the tree, that we being delivered from sin, should live in righteousness, by whose stripes ye were healed," (1 Peter 2:24). "But he was wounded for our transgressions, he was broken for our iniquities; the chastisement of our peace was upon him, and with his stripes we are healed," (Isaiah 53:5). "For the transgression of my people was he plagued," (Isaiah 53:8). "Therefore will I give him a portion with the great, and he shall divide the spoil with the strong, because he has poured out his soul unto death: and he was counted with the transgressors, and he bare the sin of many, and prayed for the trespassers," (Isaiah 53:12). "Who was delivered to death for our sins, and is risen again for our justification," (Romans 4:25). "For Christ our passover is sacrificed for us," (1 Corinthians 5:7).

3. That by his passion he pacified God, and made expiation for all our sins, "This is my beloved Son, in whom I am well pleased, hear him," (Matthew 17:5). "And walk in love, even as Christ hath loved us, and hath given himself for us to be an offering, and a sacrifice of a sweet smelling savor unto God,"

(Ephesians 5:2). "My babes, these things write I unto you, that ye sin not: and if any man sin, we have an advocate with the Father, Jesus Christ the just, and he is the reconciliation for our sins," (1 John 2:1).

4. That in his own person he fulfilled and finished all sufferings needful for our salvation. He did it once for all, "For Christ also hath once suffered for sins, the just for the unjust, that he might bring us to God," (1 Peter 3:18). "So Christ was once offered to take away the sins of many, and unto them that look for him shall he appear the second time without sin unto salvation," (Hebrews 9:28). "And every priest appeareth daily ministering, and often times offereth one manner of offering, which can never take away sins. But this man after he had offered one sacrifice for sins, sitteth forever at the right hand of God?" (Hebrews 10:11-12).

5. That the passion of Christ is a sufficient price for the sins of the whole world, "Behold the Lamb of God which taketh away the sins of the world," (John 1:29).

6. That Christ suffered extreme things for us, even the most grievous things could be imagined: As,

1. A marvelous privation of his own glory, abasing himself, that was in the form of God, to live among men, without showing that fullness of majesty and glory which was in his nature, "And now glorify me, thou Father, with thine own self, with the glory which I had with thee before the world was," (John 17:5).

2. Most base entertainment in the world, such as extreme poverty in his birth and life, "And this shall be a sign to you, ye shall find the child swaddled and laid in a manger," (Luke 2:12). "But Jesus said unto him, the foxes have holes, and the birds of the heavens have nests, but the Son of man hath not whereon to rest his head," (Matthew 8:20).

Exile to a foreign country, and flying before his enemies, "So he arose, and took the babe and his mother by night, and departed into Egypt," (Matthew 2:14). "And the Pharisees departed, and straightway gathered a counsel with the Herodians against him, that they might destroy him. But Jesus avoided with his disciples to the sea," (Mark 3:6-7). "Jesus therefore walked no more openly amongst the Jews, but went thence," (John 11:54). "Then took they up stones to cast at him, but Jesus hid himself and went out of the temple," (John 8:59).

Slanders and extreme indignities, called a Samaritan, a glutton, a seducer, a traitor; despised, mocked, buffeted, railed on, beaten, betrayed, and sold by his own servant, and that for a base price, forsaken of his own disciples, denied, and renounced by oath, falsely accused, whipped, spit upon, taken, and bound as a malefactor, and as the story of the Evangelists show.

3. Imputation of the sins of all the elect to him; so as the guilt of them was laid on him, and he sustained their person. This is a wonderful abasement, he was made sin for us, that knew no sin in himself, (2 Corinthians 5:21).

4. Fearful agonies in his very soul, arising,

1. First, from several conflicts and temptations, (Hebrews 2:18, 4:15). But especially set upon these temptations with all their fury invisibly when he was on the cross, "And hath spoiled the principalities and powers, and hath made a show of them openly, and hath triumphed over them in the same cross," (Colossians 2:15).

2. Secondly, from the pouring out of the vials of God's wrath for sin, which befell him chiefly in the garden, when he sweat blood for very anguish; and on the cross when he cried, "My God, my God, why hast thou forsaken me?"

5. A most miserable manner of death: to die as a condemned man, and condemned too both by Jews and Gentiles; to die such a cursed death, as the death of the cross, which was both by God and man designed out, as the most ignominious kind of death; and to be put to death in the midst of such malefactors, being reckoned among sinners, "Therefore will I give him a portion with the great, and he shall divide the spoil with the strong, because he hath poured out his soul unto death, and he was counted with the transgressors, and he bare the sin of many, and prayed for the trespassers," (Isaiah 53:12). And to suffer the nailing of his body, yes and the effusion of his most precious blood. These are exquisite things.

The consideration of which may serve both for

1. Instruction.

2. Information.

3. Consolation.

1. For instruction, and so it may teach us diverse duties which we should perform,

1. To Christ himself.

2. To our neighbors.

3. To ourselves.

The mediation of the passion of Christ should inflame in us a desire and resolution:

1. To acknowledge the marvelous mercies of our Savior, and to confess his praises, and to adore his name, that could be willing to suffer such things for us, "Every tongue should confess, that Jesus Christ is the Lord, unto the glory of God the Father," (Philippians 2:11). "Who is this that cometh from Edom with red garments from Bozra, he is glorious in his apparel, and walketh in his great strength. I will remember the mercies of the Lord, and the praises of the Lord, according unto the Lord hath given us, and for the great goodness toward the

house of Israel, which he hath given them according to his tender love, and according to his great mercies," (Isaiah 63:1-2,7-8).

2. To mourn affectionately for our sins, that have so pierced the Son of God, as we are taught, (Zechariah 12:12). They are the nails that pierced, and the lance that let out his heart blood. Would you not be grieved, if you had killed your own brother?

3. To sin no more, but forever to be afraid of crucifying the Son of God again, (Romans 6:6; Hebrews 10:24). But rather to live to him that died for us, and to devote both souls and bodies unto his service, "He died for all, that they which live should not henceforth live unto themselves, but unto him which died for them, and rose again," (2 Corinthians 5:15).

4. To love him with our utmost affections, and with all the sincerity of our hearts, accounting them taken, broken, given, and slain for our sakes, shall we not do this in remembrance of him? Shall we not eat the sweet flesh of this immaculate Lamb, with the sour herbs of contrition, and grief for our sins and unworthiness? Shall we not at this feast put away all leaven out of our dwellings? God forbid, we should dare to eat of this bread, or drink of this cup unworthily, and so make ourselves guilty of the blood of Christ. Rather let us all examine ourselves, and so let us eat in remembrance of him, judging ourselves, that we be not condemned of the Lord. So much of the first sort of duties.

2. Secondly, the mediation of Christ's passion should direct us, and stir us up to the care of diverse things in our carriage one toward another, and these duties are either general to all, or special to some.

There are four general duties we should learn from the passion of Christ:

1. The first is harmlessness. Seeing Christ in our passover is sacrificed for us, we should keep the feast with unleavened bread of sincerity and truth, and put away all leaven out of our dwellings; even all leaven of malice and naughtiness, all vile affections one against another, (1 Corinthians 5:7-8).

2. The second is humility. The same mind should be in us, that was in Christ Jesus; who being equal with God, was content for our sakes to make himself of no reputation, taking upon him the form of a servant; we should in lowliness of mind each esteem others better than themselves, doing nothing through strife or vainglory, looking not on our own things, but everyone also on the things of others, making ourselves equal to them of the lower sort, being of one accord, of one mind. If we would learn anything of Christ, we must learn lowliness, and meekness of him, (Philippians 2:2-9, Matthew 11:29).

3. The third is love, and that in its fervency and constancy, refusing no pains, nor dangers to show our affection to the brethren. We should walk in love, as Christ loved us, and gave himself a sacrifice of sweet smelling savor to God for us, (Ephesians 5:1-2). Yes, our lives should not be dear to us to declare our love to the brethren; but as Christ laid down his life for us, so ought we to lay down our lives for the brethren, "Hereby have we perceived love, that he laid down his life for us: therefore we ought also to lay down our lives for the brethren," (1 John 3:16).

4. The fourth is pity, and that specially to such as suffer in soul. If there are any bowels in us, the remembrance of the agony of Christ in the garden, and on the cross, should make us with more tenderness of heart pity them, that for the grief and fear of their hearts they cry out, that God their God has forsaken them. If Christ needed an angel to comfort him, what

need have these of comfort? The marvelous fear and distress Christ was in, shows that these kinds of suffering of Spirit are the most grievous distresses. So we have seen this in general.

In Ephesians 5, this marvelous love of Christ to the church shown in his passion, is used as a motive to persuade husbands to love their wives, and in all dearness of affections to cherish them, and provide for them; denying themselves, that they may profit and be content, as Christ did, when he gave himself not only to the church, but also for the church, (Ephesians 5:25). So much of the duties also to others.

3. Thirdly, the meditation of these principles about the passion of Christ should excite us to the practice and care of diverse duties that concern ourselves, as,

1. First, we should here learn to joy and glory in the cross of Christ above all things. The remembrance of the love of Christ in this, and our wonderful deliverance from the unspeakable dangers we were in, by reason of our sins, should breed in us a marvelous inward and heart exulting in this expiation of sins by the passion of Christ. In this way Paul says, "God forbid I should rejoice in anything, but the cross of Christ," (Galatians 6:14).

2. We should (while we live) have more care of our precious souls; the price paid to ransom them, should teach us their worth, and to know that they are things that must be looked to with more care than ordinary. There was more given to redeem a soul, than needed to be given to buy the whole world, yes, many worlds. We are accustomed to be exceedingly careful to keep such things, as cost dear with all circumspection; never anything cost more than a soul; and therefore nothing must be so attended as the soul, which is committed to you to preserve, until the day of Christ.

3. Thirdly, these extreme things, Christ has suffered for us, to show his love to us, should make us forever trust him, and rely only upon him, as the life of our lives, and the breath of our nostrils, so as we should always resolve with the Apostle Paul, (Galatians 2:20) that the life we now live in the flesh, we will live by the faith of the Son of God, who showed his love to us, by giving himself for us, "For Christ is to me both in life, and in death advantage," (Philippians 1:21).

4. These terrible agonies and sufferings of Christ should make us live in fear, and spend the time of our sojourning here in a singular fear to offend God anymore by our sins; yes, seeing we were to be washed in blood, before we could be clean, we should be desirous to get such purity, as that if it were possible, we might not have a spot or wrinkle of sin about us, "Pass the time of your dwelling here in fear: Knowing that ye were not redeemed with corruptible things, as silver and gold, from your vain conversation received by the traditions of the Fathers: but with the precious blood of Christ, as of a Lamb undefiled, and without spot," (1 Peter 1:17-19). "That he might sanctify it, and cleanse it by the washing of water through the word, that he might make it to himself a glorious Church, not having spot, or wrinkle, or any such thing: but that it should be holy, and without blame," (Ephesians 5:26-27).

5. We may here learn an excellent way, how to mortify sin, and destroy the power of any corruption. Look how God dealt with sin, so should we. But God used crucifying, as the best medicine to kill its force and guilt, and so should we. It is here that the term of *crucifying* is given to the mortification of sin, "For they that are Christ's have crucified the flesh with the affections, and the lusts," (Galatians 5:24). We are therefore counseled to crucify the flesh accordingly in many places of Scripture. Now that we may crucify our sins:

1. We must have them sent to the cross of Christ, force them before the tree, on which he suffered; it is such a sight as sin cannot abide. It will begin to die within a man on the sight of Christ on the cross. For, the cross of Christ accuses sin, shames sin, and by a secret virtue feeds on the very heart of sin.

2. We must make a use of sin as Christ was used, when he was made sin for us; we must lift it up, and make it naked by confession of it to God; we must pierce the hands and feet, and heart of it by godly sorrow, and application of threatenings against it, and by spiritual revenge upon it.

The hands, I say, in respect of operation, that it may work no more. The feet in respect of progression, that it may reign no longer; and the heart in respect of affection, that it may be loved no longer: we have an inward seat for concupiscence to lodge in. And in this way we should on all occasions, so especially in the preparation to the Sabbath, and when we are to keep a Passover to the Lord. That was the time chosen to crucify Christ in, and certainly it is a wonderful fit time for us to execute this work of mortification on our sins.

Lastly, this doctrine of the passion of Christ should wonderfully arm us with patience in all afflictions. The Captain of our salvation was consecrated through afflictions, "For it became him, for whom are all things, and by whom are all things, seeing that he brought many children unto glory, that he should consecrate the Prince of their salvation through affliction," (Hebrews 2:10). Though he was the Son, yet he learned obedience by the things he suffered, (Hebrews 5:8). Forasmuch as Christ has suffered for us in the flesh, we should arm ourselves with the same mind, (1 Peter 4:1). For we are called to this, and Christ suffered for us, leaving us an example, that we should follow his steps in doing well, and taking it patiently, when we suffer evil, (1 Peter 2:19-21).

Afflictions are the marks of Christ, and we should glory in it always to bear about in the body the dying of the Lord Jesus, (2 Corinthians 4:10, Galatians 6:17). And God has predestinated us, that we should be conformed to the image of his Son in sufferings, (Romans 8:29). And therefore, if we will reign with Christ, we must suffer with him, (2 Timothy 2:12). Let us therefore be fully persuaded to take up our cross also daily, and follow him, (Luke 9:23). Let us therefore also go forth to him without the camp bearing his reproach, (Hebrews 13:13). And with patience run the race that is set before us; looking to him, that being the Author and Finisher of our faith, endured such contradiction of sinners against himself; endured the cross, despised the shame, and resisted even to blood, (Hebrews 12:1-4). We should never therefore be weary, having such a pattern before us, and knowing the end God gave to him, and has promised to us, and accomplished in the experience of others of his servants; but even learn to obey God in this commandment about afflictions, as well as any other.

2. So we have considered the *uses* for instruction. The *uses* for information follow. The doctrine of the passion of Christ may inform us in diverse things, as,

1. First, concerning true felicity in its negative consideration. For inasmuch as Christ had so little to do with the world, and spent his days so without the profits and pleasures of this life, it shows that his kingdom was not of this world, and that the best treasures do not lie in these things; and besides, that one may be truly blessed, and yet be extremely destitute of these outward comforts of life.

2. Secondly, concerning the dangerousness of the doctrine of the papists. For, these principles show us that we must forever separate from them, if they persist in their heresies. For they teach us that Christ did not once for all fully

sacrifice to God, but that the sacrifice must be renewed daily in the mass, contrary to the express words of the text, "For then must he have often suffered since the foundation of the world: but now in the end of the world hath he appeared once to put away sin by the sacrifice of himself. So Christ was *once* offered to take away the sins of many," (Hebrews 9:26,28). "And every priest appeareth daily ministering, and often times offereth one manner of offering, which can never take away sins: But this man after he had offered one sacrifice for sins, sitteth forever at the right hand of God," (Hebrews 10:11-12).

And besides, they teach that men may make satisfaction to God for their sins by their own works, and by the works of the saints.

3. Thirdly, concerning the most woeful condition of wicked men that live in their sins, they may fully see how they shall speed with God by this that befell Christ. If God did not spare his only begotten Son, that was but a surety for sin, will he spare those that are principals? Would God not find out such a mercy to Christ, as to free him from such extremities; and do they trust to a mercy in God never revealed in the Word, never shown to Christ? Was Christ not able without such woeful tortures to bear the wrath of God; and do they think to be able to endure those rivers of brimstone and fire in hell?

4. Concerning a singular and new way of obedience in Christ: if we will necessarily have works of supererogation, let us acknowledge them only in Christ. For the doctrine of his passion tells us of an obedience to a commandment of God, that was not in the moral law; and that was his special submission to that singular will of his Father, in being that one should die for the people. To expiate for other men's sins, is a special kind of righteousness, not mentioned in the law.

5. Concerning the offense of the cross, though both Jews and Gentiles stumbled at this doctrine at the first; yet we see there is no reason why we should be troubled at the abasement of Christ, but rather to rejoice, and wonder at the dreadful expiation that was made to God for us in it. For in this way it behooved him to suffer, as all the Prophets from Moses have witnessed, (1 Corinthians 1:23, Luke 24:45-46). So much of the use for information.

3. The consolations follow. The doctrine of the passion of Christ is exceedingly comfortable and that both in general and particular consolations. It is generally comfortable:

1. First, in respect of the establishment of our hearts, in the assurance that Jesus of Nazareth was the true Messiah promised to the Fathers. Which may appear, if we consider but the history of his passion, inasmuch as in him were fulfilled all these signs foretold in the several ages of the old Church. The old prophecies were all accomplished in him. The scepter was now departed from Judah, foretold, (Genesis 49:10). They divided his garments, and cast lots upon his vesture, according to Psalm 22:8. They pierced his hands and feet, (Psalm 22:16). The chief builders refused him, according to Psalm 118:22). In his arraignment he was silent, and did not open his mouth, according to Isaiah 53:7. He was reckoned amongst the wicked in his death, according to Isaiah 53:12. They gave him gall and vinegar to drink, according to Psalm 69:21. He accomplished the meaning of the sacrifices in shedding his blood, and suffering without the camp, (Hebrews 9:14, 13:11-12).

2. Secondly, if we consider the effects of his passion. For, from here flows to us, and every believer,

1. First the purchase both of our souls and bodies, "For ye are bought for a price: therefore glorify God in your body, and in your spirit: for they are God's," (1 Corinthians 6:20). "So

ye my brethren are dead also to the law by the body of Christ, that ye should be unto another, even unto him, that is raised up from the dead, that we should bring forth fruit unto God," (Romans 7:4).

2. The ratification of the eternal covenant, "For where a testament is, there must also be the death of him that made the testament," (Hebrews 9:16).

3. The reconciling of us to God, "For if when we were enemies, we were reconciled to God by the death of his Son, much more being reconciled, we shall be saved by his life," (Romans 5:10). "For Christ also hath once suffered for sins: the just for the unjust, that he might bring us to God," (1 Peter 3:18).

4. The abolishing of sin, both in respect of the remission of the guilt, "The blood of Jesus Christ his Son cleanseth us from all sin," (1 John 1:7). "For this is my blood of the new testament, that is shed for many for the remission of sins," (Matthew 26:28). And sanctification against the power of it, "Knowing this, that our old man is crucified with him, that the body of sin might be destroyed, that henceforth we should not serve sin," (Romans 6:6).

5. The swallowing up of death, "So when this corruptible hath put on incorruption, and this mortal hath put on immortality: then shall be brought to pass the saying that is written: Death is swallowed up into victory," (1 Corinthians 15:54). Vanquishing him who had the power of death, freeing us that were in bondage to the fear, and that of death, "Forasmuch then as the children are partakers of flesh and blood, he also himself likewise took part with them, that he might destroy through death him that had the power of death, that is, the devil. And that he might deliver all them, which for fear of death were all their lifetime subject to bondage," (Hebrews 2:14-15). "But is now made manifest by the appearing

of our Savior Jesus Christ, who hath abolished death, and hath brought life and immortality unto light through the Gospel," (2 Timothy 1:10).

6. Liberty to enter into the most holy place of heaven, by a new and living way, "Neither by the blood of goats and calves, but by his own blood entered he once unto the holy place, and obtained eternal redemption for us," (Hebrews 9:12). "Seeing therefore brethren, that by the blood of Jesus we may be bold to enter into the holy place," (Hebrews 10:19).

3. Thirdly, if we consider the order of priesthood, of which he was in offering this sacrifice. He was a priest after the order of Melchizedek, and not after Aaron, "The Lord sware and will not repent, thou art a Priest forever after the order of Melchizedek," (Psalm 110:4; *cf.* Hebrews 7, the entire chapter).

Of all the priests that were types of Christ, Melchizedek was the most lively and noble type, and most comfortable things in Christ were shadowed out:

1. The first was his dignity. He was so a Priest, as he was a King also, able to feed and nourish the most mighty on earth, as the King of Salem did Abraham.

2. The second was the efficacy of his priesthood, noted in two admirable benefits flowing from his obedience and passion, viz. Righteousness and peace: Righteousness, for he is the Lord our righteousness; Peace, in that he fully pacified God's anger for our sins, as our atonement, and so he was indeed that King of *Zedech*, that is, *of righteousness*: and of Salem, that is, of peace.

3. The third was the eternity of his priesthood; he is a priest forever, he does not die, as the sons of Levi did, nor does the efficacy of his priesthood ever cease. The Holy Spirit of purpose conceals the mention of the birth and death of Melchizedek, so that he might be the fuller type of Christ, who

had no father as man, nor mother as God; and of his days there is no end; which last thing is the special consolation, for which I alleged this type. There is no time in which we can lack the benefit of Christ's sacrifice, if we have access to God, and the throne of his grace; and this rather because God has sworn and will not repent, (Psalm 110:4). So much for all this in general.

In particular, there are many excellent comforts that may be raised from the passion of Christ, for,

1. First, here we may gather a matchless testimony, and undoubted, of the infinite love of God to man, in that he spared not his own Son, but gave him to the death for us, "For God so loved the world, that he hath given his only begotten Son, that whosoever believeth in him should not perish, but have everlasting life," (John 3:16). "In this appeared the love of God toward us, because God sent his only begotten Son into the world, that we might live through him," (1 John 4:9). Which may likewise assure us that there is nothing that can be good for us, but he will certainly give it to us also, "Who spared not his own Son, but gave him for us all to death, how shall he not with him give us all things also?" (Romans 8:32).

2. Secondly, shall we ever doubt our freedom from condemnation, that know here what a price was paid for discharge of our debts by such a surety? How can we be so vilely infected with unbelief, as to fear arresting, or imprisonment, or undoing, when all is in Christ so fully and exquisitely satisfied to the very uttermost farthing? How could the surety have ever escaped such justice in God? Such malice in men, and devils, the sergeants and jailors? If he had not most abundantly paid all could be demanded.

3. Thirdly, what an encouragement may this be to believe what Christ says to us? Was he not a faithful Witness and Teacher, that sealed his doctrine with his blood? Great

therefore is the infallibility of the Gospel, that truth which is according to godliness, and to be received with all full assurance without wavering or fear," (Revelation 1:5).

4. Fourthly, shall his example not comfort us in all trials, especially when we suffer the most extreme things which can befall us in this life? What are those to the sufferings of Christ? And with what compassion will he receive us in affliction, that was so afflicted himself? (Isaiah 63:1-9).

And in particular, it may ease in pains and in death itself, to remember the sorrows of Christ, especially considering that from there flows a virtue to help us in all our pangs and distresses, in life and death.

5. Lastly, there are many particular comforts that may be gathered from the manner of his suffering, and diverse particularities in them; as,

1. He suffered in Jerusalem, and so both fulfilled the types of the Old Testament. For there was Isaac offered up, and there the sacrifices were slain, and also signified to us, that he had obtained for us the vision of eternal peace, which the name Jerusalem imports.

2. Secondly, he suffered the first part of his chief passion in a garden, to comfort us in the abolishing of the first sin, which was committed in a garden, and imputed to Christ.

3. Thirdly, he was betrayed, taken, bound, and forsaken, and all for us. He was betrayed, to expiate our treason in Adam: he was taken to restore us captives. He was bound that we might be loosed. He was forsaken of all, even of his own best disciples, to let us know that he alone performed the work of satisfaction and redemption for us, (Isaiah 63:3).

4. Fourthly, he was arraigned and condemned both by Jews and Gentiles in the consistory of the priests, and at the tribunal of Pilate, thereby to notify both to Jews and Gentiles,

that he was given to sacrifice for sins of both, and to signify that he was truly Messiah, or Shiloh, because now the scepter was departed from Judah, (Genesis 49:10).

5. His silence to the most accusations shows: 1. That he was a greater person than he that judged him. 2. Secondly, that he fulfilled the Scriptures, that said he did not open his mouth, (Isaiah 53:7). 3. That he suffered for our evil words, but especially it assures us, that he suffered them as our surety, in that he endured the imputation of such monstrous crimes, and yet held his peace.

6. He was whipped, and crowned with thorns; he was whipped, to deliver us from both spiritual, corporeal, and eternal scourges that were due to us.

The crown of thorns may signify:

1. That he expiated our ambition in Adam.

2. That he might merit for us an eternal crown.

3. That he would gather a kingly people out of the most thorny and hurtful nations, which as a crown should compass God about in serving and honoring him.

4. That he had born our thorny cares, and therefore we should cast all our cares upon him.

7. He was clothed with a purple garment, and a reed in his hand, which both signified that he was a King, though they did it in scorn. His purple garment shows that he was that great Warrior, which was forespoken of, when they said, "Who is this that comes from Edom with red garments?" (Isaiah 63:1-7). The reed was comfortable in two ways: for first it showed that this was he that should break the serpent's head: for a reed is the most mortal thing to a serpent, as the learned record, and with that they were used to kill them; and besides a reed, as by a pen he blotted out the handwriting in a debt book, that was against us.

8. He suffered in Golgotha, a place of dead men's bones, in which the most notorious offenders suffered their punishment, so that he might raise up the banner of justification, even in the very place of contamination and damnation.

9. He was unclothed, and made naked to satisfy for the sin of our first parents, who were spoiled of the garment of innocence; and to deliver us from sin and mortality, of which the garments of skin given to our parents, were a monument; and perhaps to show how we should enter into heaven, *viz.* as Adam did into paradise naked in body, but clothed in soul with innocence and immortality: but chiefly to expiate for our shameful wickedness before God.

10. He was hung on a tree, so that as death by the tree entered into the world, so on a tree it should be destroyed, and life brought back again. And besides in this Christ answered the type in Isaac's offering up, and the brazen serpent lifted up on high, (John 3:14) and that Christ lifted up in the air, might overcome the Prince of the air, and all his spiritual wickedness, (Colossians 2:15). And that he might bear the curse of the law, being in that kind of death made a special curse for us, (Galatians 3:13-14).

11. He drank gall and vinegar, in which he both fulfilled the Scriptures, "For they gave me gall in my meat, and in my thirst they gave me vinegar to drink," (Psalm 69:21). And as the second Adam bore the punishment of the first Adam's offense in tasting the juice of the forbidden fruit.

12. The nailing of his hands and feet assures us of the cancelling of the handwriting of ordinances that was against us; both of the dissolution of all ceremonial agreements, and of the full cancelling of the bond moral for so much as concerns the forfeiture that lay upon us, (Colossians 2:14).

CHAPTER 21:
Of Christ's Intercession

We have considered the expiation of sins. The third part of the priesthood of Christ follows, and that is the intercession of Christ: concerning which there are four principles.

1. That Christ at the right hand of God makes intercession for us, "Who shall condemn? It is Christ, which is dead, yea, or rather, which is risen again, who is also at the right hand of God, and maketh request also for us," (Romans 8:34). "Wherefore he is able also perfectly to save them, that come unto God by him, seeing he ever liveth to make intercession for them."

2. That we have no other intercessor in heaven but Christ, "For there is one God, and one Mediator between God and man, which is the man Christ Jesus; Who gave himself a ransom for all men to be a testimony in due time," (1 Timothy 2:5-6). "And when he saw that there was no man, he wondered that there was no intercessor: therefore his arm saved it, and his righteousness itself sustained it," (Isaiah 59:16).

3. That the intercession of Christ is perpetual, he so does it once, as he will never fail to do it in all ages, "For the law maketh men high priests which have infirmity: but the word of the oath, that was since the law, maketh the Son, who was consecrated forevermore," (Hebrews 7:25,28).

4. That he makes intercession only for the elect, "I pray for them: I pray not for the world, but for them which thou hast given me: for they are thine," (John 17:9).

Now for the explanation of these principles, three things must be opened.

1. The first is the acceptation of the word *intercession*: for it signifies:

-Sometimes the prayers which the godly make in the name of Christ the Intercessor, to turn away God's judgments from their brethren in this world, and so it is taken, "I exhort therefore, that first of all supplications, prayers, intercessions, and giving of thanks be made for all men," (1 Timothy 2:1).

-Sometimes the complaints that men make or pretend to make against the faults of others. In this way Elias made intercession against Israel, (Romans 11:2). And the Jews made intercession against Paul, (Acts 25:24). But usually it signifies that part of the mediation of Christ, in which he appears before God to prevent or pacify his displeasure towards the elect.

2. The second part is, how many ways Christ makes intercession for us, and so there are seven distinct things in the intercession of Christ: For,

1. First, he presents himself before God in his merits tendering his sacrifice for our satisfaction, "For Christ is not entered into the holy places that are made with hands, which are similitudes of the true sanctuary: but is entered into the very heaven, to appear now in the sight of God for us," (Hebrews 9:24). And so pacifying God toward us, (Jeremiah 30:31).

2. He prayed, and still does pray for us. All his prayers on earth were a part of his intercession, and he still prays for us in heaven, "Who is also at the right hand of God, and maketh request also for us," (Romans 8:34). "Wherefore he is able also perfectly to save them that come unto God by him, seeing he ever liveth to make intercession for them," (Hebrews 7:25).

3. He offers up our prayers and praises to God, "That he should offer with the prayers of all saints upon the golden altar, which is before the throne. And the smoke of the odors with

the prayers of the saints went up before God and out of the angel's hand," (Revelation 8:3-4). And so, all our good works, "In the body of his flesh through death, to make you holy and unblameable, and without fault in his sight," (Colossians 1:22).

4. He undertakes for us before God, and gives his word for us, that we being mindful of reconciliation through him, shall eschew sin by his grace, and not provoke God anymore, as we have done. This work is a necessary part of the office of an intercessor, "I have declared thy name unto the men, which thou gavest me out of the world, thine they were, and thou gavest them me, and they have kept thy word," (John 17:6). "O righteous Father, the world hath also not known thee, but I have known thee, and these have known that thou hast sent me. And I have declared unto them thy name, and will declare it, that the love wherewith thou hast loved me, may be in them, and I in them," (John 17:25-26).

5. He pleads our cause as an advocate, and removes and nonsuits all accusations which men or devils may make against us to God, (Romans 8:34 as before). "My babes, these things write I unto you, that ye sin not: and if any man sin, we have an advocate with the Father: Jesus Christ the just," (1 John 2:1).

6. He pours out on us the spirit of intercession, which causes us after an unutterable manner to make our moans and requests to God, "Likewise the spirit also helpeth our infirmities: for we know not what to pray as we ought: but the Spirit itself maketh request for us with sighs, which cannot be expressed," (Romans 8:26). So, "For ye have not received the spirit of bondage to fear again: but ye have received the spirit of adoption, whereby we cry Abba, Father," (Romans 8:15). "And because ye are sons, God hath sent forth the Spirit of his Son into your hearts, which crieth Abba, Father," (Galatians 4:6-7).

7. He sprinkles his blood on us, by application of his merits to us, which cries and makes intercession for us, "And to Jesus the mediator of the New Testament, and to the blood of sprinkling, that speaketh better things than that of Abel," (Hebrews 12:24).

3.The third is, in which nature he makes intercession? I answer, in both. For however we consider the divine nature of Christ, Christ is then equal with the Father, and the same in essence, and so it cannot fitly be said that Christ requests anything of the Father; yet if we respect the person of Christ in his divine nature, as it is personally united to his human in the dispensation of grace, as voluntarily he has undertaken for us. So, it is no more inconvenient to pray for us, than it is to take on him the form of a servant for us; and the office of a mediator to which belongs this work of praying.

The use of all this may be, first for confutation of the papists, who most sacrilegiously dishonor the intercession of Christ, by substituting secondary intercessors. The office is bestowed only on the King's Son, and they most injuriously would employ the King's servants. We know no master of requests, but Jesus Christ; nor does it help them that they say they have Mediators of intercession, but not of redemption, but only Christ. For they acknowledge and do not only beg the prayers, but the merits too of the saints to purge away their sins, and supply their needs, they make them mediators of redemption also.

Secondly, for instruction, and so it should teach us:

1. To imitate this part of the priesthood of Christ, both by praying to God for our brethren, and for all sorts of men, though they are our enemies, (1 Timothy 2:1) and also by making peace and keeping it, as much as is possible among men. "Blessed are the peacemakers," for this makes them like

the Son of God, (Matthew 5:7) and seeing the saints shall judge the world, they should put an end the quarrels among the brethren, if it may be.

2. Secondly, to live so, as Christ may have credit by us, in giving his word for us. Has Christ undertaken for us to God, and shall we not be careful to the uttermost of our power to be such as he has promised to be for us, we shall be, (John 17:10, 18-19).

3. To pray and give thanks much, and so to do all the good we can, seeing it shall all be presented to God by Christ, (Colossians 1:22, Revelation 8:3-4).

4. To establish ourselves in the full assurance of faith, seeing all our imperfections are covered in Christ's intercession, and we may approach God by this new and living way, and be sure of heaven also, even to come within the veil, when we die, (Hebrews 10:19).

Thirdly, for consolation: for we may and ought to be much refreshed, if we consider that by the intercession of Christ:

1. The favor of God is established upon us, and God is kept quiet from being provoked against us; God and we are now through him all one, (John 17:21).

2. The compassion of God is implored in the times of distress and affliction, (Zechariah 1:16).

3. The devil is restrained, he cannot hurt us, either by tempting or accusing; our faith shall be kept, that is does not fail, (Zechariah 3:3, Romans 8:34, Luke 22:32).

4. Our sins which we daily commit, are forgiven us, he being an earnest advocate to plead for us, (1 John 2:12).

5. We shall be protected against the hatred of the world, "I have given them thy word, and the world hath hated them, because they are not of the world, as I am not of the

world. I pray not that thou shouldest take them out of the world, but that thou keep them from evil," (John 17:14-16).

6. Our prayers and suits shall be all presented and obtained, (Revelation 8:4).

7. We shall be kept from evil, and preserved to the end, until we are perfected from all sins and needs, "And now am I no more in the world, these are in the world, and I come to thee: holy Father keep them in thy name, even them whom thou hast given me, that they may be one as we are," (John 17:11). "I pray not that thou shouldest take them out of the world, but that thou keep them from evil," (John 17:15). "I in them, and thou in me, that they may be made perfect in one," (John 17:23).

8. We have assured hope of the glory of heaven, and to dwell in the most holy place, that is, within the veil, "Seeing therefore brethren, that by the blood of Jesus we may be bold to enter into the holy place," (Hebrews 10:19). "Wherefore he is able also perfectly to save them that come unto God by him, seeing he ever liveth to make intercession for them," (Hebrews 7:25). "Father, I will that they which thou hast given me, be with me, even where I am, that they may behold my glory which thou hast given me; for thou lovedst me before the foundation of the world," (John 17:24). "If ye then be risen with Christ, seek those things which are above, where Christ sitteth at the right hand of God," (Colossians 3:1).

9. We shall be blessed and given with all needful blessings in the meantime, (Hebrews 12:24).

10. All this is the more comfortable, because he lives ever to make request for us. There is no cessation of this office, but at all times we may have its benefits, (John 17:20). "Wherefore he is able also perfectly to save them that come unto God by him, seeing he ever liveth to make intercession for them," (Hebrews 7:25).

CHAPTER 22:
Of the Regal Office of Christ

We have considered the priestly office of Christ, his regal office follows. And here first I will plainly lay down the principles, and prove them. And then for more evidence methodically for an explanation I will show the parts of his office in this, and then lastly make uses of all of it.

There are seven things to be believed concerning Christ, which belong to his regal office.

1. First, that he overcame sin, death, the grave, and hell, and rose again from the dead, and ascended into heaven, and sits at the right hand of God in majesty.

That he is risen from the dead, these places are evident to keep in our memories, "And declared mightily to be the Son of God, touching the Spirit of sanctification by the resurrection from the dead," (Romans 1:4). "Who was delivered to death for our sins, and is risen again for our justification," (Romans 4:25). "Then shall be brought to pass the saying that is written, death is swallowed up in victory," (1 Corinthians 15:54). "And saw two angels in white, sitting the one at the head, the other at the feet, where the body of Jesus had lain," (John 20:12). "But he said unto them, be not afraid, ye seek Jesus of Nazareth, which hath been crucified: he is risen, he is not here, behold the place where they put him," (Mark 16:6). "Finally, he appeared unto the eleven, as they sat together, and reproved them of their unbelief, and hardness of heart, because they believed not them which had seen him, being risen up again," (Mark 16:14). "Remember that Jesus Christ made of the seed of David, was raised again from the dead, according to my Gospel," (2 Timothy 2:8).

That he ascended into heaven, these places may suffice to prove it, "So after the Lord had spoken unto them, he was received into heaven, and sat at the right hand of God," (Mark 16:19). "And it came to pass that as he blessed them, he departed from them, and was carried up into heaven," (Luke 24:51). "And when he had spoken these things, while they beheld, he was taken up; for a cloud took him up out of their sight," (Acts 1:9). "Wherefore he saith, when he ascended up on high: he led captivity captive, and gave gifts unto men. Now in that he ascended, what is it, but that he had also descended first into the lowest parts of the earth. He that descended, is even the same that ascended far above all heavens, that he might fill all things," (Ephesians 4:8-10).

That he sits at the right hand of God, these places prove, "So after the Lord had spoken unto them, he was received into heaven, and sat at the right hand of God," (Mark 16:19). "Unto which also of the angels said he at any time: Sit at my right hand, till I make thine enemies thy footstool," (Hebrews 1:9). "Now of the things which we have spoken, this is the sum, that we have such an high Priest that sitteth at the right hand of the throne of the majesty in heaven," (Hebrews 8:1). "Which he wrought in Christ when he raised him from the dead, and set him at his right hand in the heavenly places. Far above all principalities and power, and might, and dominion, and every name that is named, not in this world only, but also in that that is to come," (Ephesians 1:20-21). "If ye then be risen with Christ, seek those things which are above, where Christ sitteth at the right hand of God," (Colossians 3:1).

2. That Christ who purchased the church by his blood, is appointed of God to be the King, and head of the church, and Prince over the people of God, having all power in his own hands, "Even I have set my King upon Zion mine holy

mountain," (Psalm 2:6). "And Jesus came and spake unto them saying, All power is given unto me in heaven and in earth," (Matthew 28:18). "Jesus knowing that the Father had given all things into his hands, and that he was come from God, and went to God," (John 13:3). "And he is the head of the body of the Church, he is the beginning and the firstborn of the dead, that in all things he might have the preeminence," (Colossians 1:18). "And he hath upon his garment, and upon his thigh a name written; the King of Kings, and Lord of Lords," (Revelation 19:16).

3. That he is likewise appointed to be the Lawgiver to the church, and the Judge of the whole world, "There is one law-giver, which is able to save and to destroy: who art thou that judgest another man?" (James 4:12). "For the Father judgeth no man, but hath committed all judgment unto the Son," (John 5:22). "And hath given him power also to execute judgment, in that he is the son of man," (John 5:27). "And he commanded us to preach unto the people, and to testify that it is he that is ordained of God, a judge of quick and dead," (Acts 10:42). "Because he hath appointed a day, in the which he will judge the world in righteousness, by that man whom he hath appointed of which he hath given him an assurance unto all men, in that he hath raised him from the dead," (Acts 17:31). "I charge ye therefore before God, and before the Lord Jesus Christ, which shall judge the quick and the dead at his appearing, and in his kingdom," (2 Timothy 4:1).

4. That his government extends to the people of all nations, "Ask of me, and I will give thee the heathen for thine inheritance, and the ends of the earth for thy possession," (Psalm 2:8). "And Jesus came and spake unto them, saying: All power is given unto me in heaven and in earth," (Matthew 28:18). "That at the name of Jesus should every knee bow, both

of things in heaven, and things in earth, and things under the earth. And that every tongue should confess, that Jesus Christ is the Lord, unto the glory of God the Father," (Philippians 2:10-11).

5. That his kingdom is not of this world, but a spiritual and celestial kingdom, "Jesus answered, my kingdom is not of this world; if my kingdom were of this world, my servants would surely fight, that I should not be delivered to the Jews; but now is my kingdom not from hence," (John 18:36). "For the kingdom of God is not meat, nor drink, but righteousness, and peace, and joy in the Holy Ghost," (Romans 14:17).

6. That he will be with his people to the end of the world, "Teaching them to observe all things, whatsoever I have commanded you: and lo I am with you always until the end of the world, Amen," (Matthew 28:20).

7. This his kingdom is an everlasting kingdom, "And he shall reign over the house of Jacob forever, and of his kingdom shall be no end," (Luke 1:33). "Wherefore seeing we receive a kingdom which cannot be shaken, let us have grace, whereby we may so serve God, that we may please him with reverence and fear," (Hebrews 12:28). "And in the days of these kings shall the God of heaven set up a kingdom, which shall never be destroyed, and this kingdom shall not be given to another people, but it shall break and destroy all these kingdoms, and it shall stand forever," (Daniel 2:44). "And he gave him dominion, and honor, and a kingdom, that all people, nations, and languages should serve him; his dominion is an everlasting dominion, which shall never be taken away, and his kingdom shall never be destroyed," (Daniel 7:14).

Objection. Against this last principle may be objected the words of the Apostle, "Then shall be the end, when he hath delivered up the kingdom to God, even the Father, when he hath put down all rule, and all authority, and power," (1 Corinthians 15:24). And therefore after that time it seems he shall reign no more.

Solution: For an answer to this, we must know that Christ shall not then cease to reign, but only cease to reign after the same manner he does now. That manner of administration, which he now uses in gathering and preserving his church shall then cease, there shall be then no need of it. So we have covered the principles.

Now for the explanation, that we may more distinctly conceive of this office of Christ, as King, we must consider of four things in it.

1. The victory over the enemies that opposed his title.

2. His kingly glory, with which he was qualified and prepared for government.

3. His taking possession of the kingdom.

4. His administration, after he had possession.

1. For the first, Christ fought for his kingdom, and most victoriously overcame the devil, sin, death, and hell, and rescued his subjects from their thralldom, (1 Corinthians 15:54-55, Colossians 2:15, Hebrews 2:14). And this victory he accomplished, and proclaimed in his resurrection from the dead.

2. For the second: the regal glory of Christ consisted in two things: the first was the glorification of his human nature. And the second was his triumph over his enemies.

1. The glorification of his human nature contained,

1. The deposition of all the infirmities accompanying our nature, which he undertook for our sakes; so as he now ceased to hunger, or thirst, or be weary, or feel any pain, or grief, nor could he suffer anymore, or die.

2. The perfecting of his human nature, with all the degrees of celestial gifts and endowments could possibly befall a created nature, both in body and mind. His very body was glorified, surpassing the sun in the firmament, for splendor and brightness.

2. Now for the triumph of Christ, he acted it two ways;

1. In those frequent manifestations after his resurrection for the 40 days he was pleased to abide on earth.

2. In that most glorious ascension riding in the chariot of triumph up into heaven, leading with him captivity captive.

3. The third thing is, his taking possession of his kingdom, and this he did, when he sat down at the right hand of the majesty of God, and was exalted above all that is named, and had power over all things given him of his Father.

4. The fourth thing is, his administration of the kingdom, of which he is now possessed; and this has in it four things:

1. The calling and gathering together both of Jews and Gentiles belonging to the election of God, (Romans 8:20, Ephesians 4:11-12, Isaiah 11:11-12).

2. The prescribing of laws, as the only Lawgiver of the church, and this he does when he propounds unto his subjects the rules both of believing and living by the word and ministry of the same, adding thereunto the work of the Spirit, writing his laws upon their hearts, (James 4:12, Jeremiah 31:33, 2 Corinthians 3:17-18).

3. The donation of gifts, enabling men to the kingdom of God, (Ephesians 4:8, Philippians 1:29).

4. The execution of justice, and so he does justice,

1. Among his own subjects, and so he does them justice,

1. In justifying them from their sins, in acquitting them and pronouncing them absolved from all the sentences of God's justice given out against them.

2. By distributing rewards among them, both in spiritual and temporal things.

3. By keeping them in their bonds, and preserving them in the fear of God, and a just course of life.

2. Against his enemies, whom he either restrains, or subdues: he restrains them by setting them their bounds, which they may not pass; by infatuating their counsels, and by being a wall of brass about his own. He subdues them either by converting them, and so making them come in, and do him homage, or else by confounding them, which he begins partly by outward judgments, partly by induration, as delivering them up to a reprobate sense, and accomplishing it in their miserable ends, casting them into utter darkness.

This administration of his kingdom he executes, partly in this life, and partly in the world to come: the one is his kingdom of grace, the other of glory; what is but begun here, is fully made complete in that other world.

The uses of the regal office of Christ follow, and those are partly for instruction, partly for consolation.

1. First, for instruction, and we should learn,

1. To ascribe all glory, and dominion to him forever, we should so admire the greatness and majesty of our King, as our hearts should be most affectionately moved to his continual praises. Let the people praise you, O God, yes, let all the people praise you; O sing praises to our God, sing praises, sing praises with understanding, (Psalm 47:6-7, Revelation 1:5). "Saying with a loud voice, worthy is the lamb, that was killed to receive power, and riches, and wisdom, and strength, and honor, and glory, and praise. And all the creatures which are in heaven, and

on the earth, and under the earth, and in the sea, and all that are in them heard I saying; Praise, and honor, and glory, and power be unto him, that sitteth upon the throne, and unto the Lamb forevermore," (Revelation 5:12-14). And to this end we should learn,

2. To pray, that God would give us the Spirit of wisdom and revelation, that the eyes of our understanding may be enlightened to discern the working of his mighty power, which he wrought in Christ; when he raised him from the dead, and set him at his own right hand in heavenly places far above all principalities, and powers, and every name that is named, not only in this world, but also in that which is to come; and has put all things under his feet, and made him head over all things belonging to the Church, (Ephesians 1:17-23). And with all this we should stir up ourselves,

3. To pray daily, that his kingdom may come, that the people that yet are in darkness, may be converted; and that his glory may shine more and more in those that have submitted themselves to his scepter, And to this end, that the ordinances of his kingdom, especially the preaching of the Gospel may run with power, and mightily conquer and enlarge the bounds of his kingdom; and that all opposite kingdoms may be subverted, as is that of Antichrist, especially that his kingdom of glory may be hastened on us. And for our own parts we should everyone be ready,

4. To send our Lamb to the Ruler of the earth, (Isaiah 16:1) to tender our homage, and offer our service, and testify our allegiance with all humility, and thankfulness unto this King of Kings, the Lord our mighty Redeemer, and throughout the course of our lives.

5. To bow at the name of Jesus, and to fear him, that is a great King above all gods, and has a name above all names: to

confess his sovereignty, and submit to his government, and to tremble before him, and to think of him with all reverence, (Philippians 2:9-11, Psalm 2:10-11).

6. And to come willingly at all the times of the public assembly of his armies in holy beauty, we should all flock to the colors of the King, and never give over the care of assembling ourselves in the courts of our God; but with all gladness go up to the house of the Lord, the courts of the King, the place of his holy presence, where he sits in his throne amongst us, (Psalm 110:3).

7. To seek to Christ in all our necessities, seeing he is so exalted that now he is able to help us in all times of need according to the riches of his glory.

8. To be tender, and zealous for the glory and honor of Christ: shall our hearts not rise at the dishonor of our King?

9. To observe whatsoever he commands, in nothing refusing him, that speaks from heaven, "Teaching them to observes all things whatsover I have commanded you," (Matthew 28:20). "See that ye despise not him that speaketh; for if they escaped not, which refused him, that spake on earth; much more shall we not escape, if we turn away from him, that speaketh from heaven," (Hebrews 12:25).

10. To seek those things that are above, where he sitteth at the right hand of God, and to have our conversation in heaven, since as subjects of his kingdom we are freemen of the new Jerusalem, the metropolis of his kingdom. "But our conversation is in heaven, from whence we look for the Savior, even the Lord Jesus Christ," (Philippians 3:20). "If then ye be risen with Christ, seek those things which are above, where Christ sitteth at the right hand of God," (Colossians 3:1).

11. To dwell securely, as acknowledging we have secure protection in his service, and not to be afraid of anything that

may cause us fear, "Behold, the days come, saith the Lord, that I will raise unto David a righteous branch, and a King shall reign and prosper, and shall execute judgment and justice in the earth. In his days Judah shall be saved, and Israel shall dwell safely, and this is the name whereby they shall call him; The Lord our righteousness," (Jeremiah 23:5-6).

12. To carry ourselves as the servants of the King. His subjects should differ in their manners from all other nations; and his servants should order themselves so, as may become his honor. And in this way we should always resist to our power the kingdom of darkness, and set ourselves to overcome the world, and as conquerors to deny ourselves in the affection to the pleasures of the world; and not to live out our lives from the fear of the disgrace of the world, knowing it is honor enough to be such a King's servant; and out of fear even of death itself, as knowing our deliverance by the victory, which our Savior had over death; and the assurance that he will come again, and make our vile bodies like to his glorious body.

And as this may teach men in general, so there are diverse things to be urged from here upon particular people, as,

1. First, kings, judges, and rulers of the people should take notice of this, and do their homage, and bring their presents to this King of all Kings, (Psalm 68:29) and seeing they are but his vicegerents, they should be learned in the laws of his kingdom, and get wisdom to carry themselves so, as may become those that represent his person, not daring to oppose the government of Christ, or to set themselves to oppress his subjects, (Psalm 2:10-11).

2. Secondly, ministers should especially stir up themselves to mind this great work of separating men from the world, to the Kingdom of Christ.

3. Thirdly, private Christians must take heed of judging one another: for all judgment is committed to the Son, and he is the only supreme Judge and Lawgiver; and therefore the Apostle James infers, we ought not to judge our brothers.

4. Fourthly, such as have parted with their friends by death, must not sorrow for them that are gone, as men without hope, seeing the kingdom of God is come upon them, and they are with the Lord, and their dead bodies shall Christ bring with him in his coming, therefore they should not shame the government of Christ by the ignorance hereof, but comfort themselves with these things, (1 Thessalonians 4:13).

Secondly, this may serve for wonderful consolation to the godly, and that two ways,

1. The children of Zion may rejoice in their King, "Let Israel rejoice in him that made him, and let the children of Zion rejoice in their King," (Psalm 149:2). If they consider their wonderful happiness, in being subject to such a King, as

1. Was chosen and appointed by God himself immediately, "Even I have set my King upon Zion mine holy mountain," (Psalm 2:6-8).

2. Was qualified with gifts above all his fellows, even above all the men on earth, or angels in heaven, (Psalm 45:2).

3. Is independent: his subjects are not charged with supporting or defending him, but he defends and maintains them, (Isaiah 9:7).

4. Is always present with his subjects, "And lo, I am with you always until the end of the world, Amen," (Matthew 28:20).

5. Is head of all principalities and powers, and has all honor and power given to him in heaven and earth, rules over all nations, people, and languages, (Colossians 2:9, Daniel 7:13, 14:27).

6. Cannot die, but lives forever.

7. They ought exceedingly to rejoice, if they consider the privileges they have in being subjects in the kingdom of Christ: for thereby,

1. They have the favor and presence of God with them; his covenant of peace, and his sanctuary with them, (Ezekiel 37:26-27).

2. They have great dignity, they are made Kings themselves, a royal nation: they are princes of the people, even all the people of the God of Abraham, (Revelation 1:6, 1 Peter 2:9).

3. They have royal entertainment, and are daily feasted of their King, daily banquets in the Word and sacraments, Christ supping with them, (Revelation 3) yes, giving his own body for meat, and his own blood for drink, (Isaiah 25:6).

4. They dwell safely, and find shelter and succor in all distresses, (Isaiah 25:4, Ezekiel 34:25). Michael, the great prince stands for the children of the people, (Daniel 12:1).

5. Their King is exalted to the most supreme honor, and therefore is able to preserve them wonderfully; and promised before he was exalted, that he would provide them a place, (John 14:2).

CHAPTER 23:
Of the Church

"And hath made all things subject under his feet, and hath appointed him over all things to be the head of the Church," (Ephesians 1:22).

We have considered the means of grace, the subject of grace follows, and that is the church. The church is the whole multitude of men elected to eternal life by God in Christ. Concerning the church, there are these principles:

1. First, that it is a company of men separate from the world, gathered by the voice of Christ. The Scripture full makes a difference between the world and the Church; and the word signifies such, as are gathered together by the voice of God's criers. "I pray for them, I pray not for the world, but for them which thou hast given me: for they are thine," (John 17:9). "I have given them thy Word, and the world hath hated them, because they are not of the world, as I am not of the world," (John 17:14).

2. Secondly, that she is one, "There is one body, and one Spirit, even as ye are called in one hope of your salvation," (Ephesians 4:4). "But my dove is alone, and my undefiled, she is the only daughter of her mother, and she is dear to her that bare her," (Song of Solomon 6:8). "There is neither Jew, nor Gentile, there is neither bond nor free, there is neither male nor female, for ye are all one in Jesus Christ," (Galatians 3:28).

And the church is one, as in many other respects: so because all the godly are mystically united in one body, "So we being many are one body in Christ, and everyone one another's members," (Romans 12:5). "But speaking the truth in love, may grow up into him in all things, which is the head, even Christ: From whom the whole body fitly joined together and compacted by that which every joint supplieth, according to the effectual working in the measure of every part, maketh increase of the body unto the edifying of itself in love," (Ephesians 4:15-16).

3. Thirdly, that she is knit to Christ her head by an indissoluble union, "And he is the head of the body of the Church, he is the beginning, and the firstborn of the dead, that in all things he might have the preeminence," (Colossians 1:18). "And holdeth not the head, of which all the body furnished and knit together by joints and hands, increaseth with the increasing of God," (Colossians 2:19). "Now ye are the body of Christ, and members for your part," (1 Corinthians 12:27). "And hath made all things subject under his feet, and hath appointed him over all things to be the head to the Church, Which in his body, even the fullness of him that filleth all in all things," (Ephesians 1:22-23). So as she is truly bone of his bone, and flesh of his flesh, "For we are members of his body, of his flesh and of his bones," (Ephesians 5:30).

One with Christ, not in nature as the Trinity is one; nor in person, as the two natures in Christ, but in spirit, "Hereby know we that we dwell in him, and he in us, because he hath given us of his Spirit," (John 4:13). For the Spirit of the Son dwells in us.

4. Fourthly, that she is holy, "That he might make it unto himself a glorious Church, not having spot or wrinkle, or any such thing, but that it should be holy and without blame," (Ephesians 5:27). "But ye are a chosen generation, a royal priesthood, an holy nation, a peculiar people, that ye should shew forth the virtues of him that hath called you out of darkness into his marvelous light," (1 Peter 2:9). "And they shall

take the kingdom of the saints of the most high, and possess the kingdom forever, and forever and ever," (Daniel 7:18). And so she is holy,

1. By separation from the world, in that the godly are consecrated to holy uses: they are holy by calling.

2. By inchoation of true holiness in nature, and practice, "Not by the works of righteousness which we had done, but according to his mercy he saved us, by the washing of the new birth, and the renewing of the Holy Ghost," (Titus 3:5).

3. By imputation of Christ's holiness being washed in his blood, "By the which will we are sanctified, even by the offering of the body of Jesus Christ once made," (Hebrews 10:10).

4. By consummation of all holiness in the other world.

5. Fifthly, she is Catholic (*i.e.* universal): this is one of the articles of the creed: the church is Catholic in three respects:

1. In respect of time, all the godly being members of this one body, though they live in all the several ages since the world began.

2. In respect of place, because all the just both in heaven and earth are all of this one body, "That in the dispensation of the fullness of the times he might gather together in one all things, both which are in heaven, and which are in earth, even in Christ," (Ephesians 1:10). And so from all parts of the world is the church gathered, all the particular churches in the world are but members of this church universal.

3. In respect of persons, because it is gathered especially since Christ, out of all nations, there being no difference put in respect of men's outward condition, "And they sung a new song saying, Thou art worthy to take the book, and to open the seals thereof, because thou wast killed, and hast redeemed us to God

by thy blood, out of every kindred, and tongue, and people, and nation. And hast made us unto our God kings and priests, and we shall reign on earth," (Revelation 5:9-10). "There is neither Jew nor Grecian, there is neither bond nor free; there is neither male nor female: for ye are all one in Christ Jesus," (Galatians 3:28).

6. Sixthly, that she is militant, that is, she is in this life exposed to crosses, and afflictions, and temptations, and oppositions, "I have fought a good fight, and have finished my course: I have kept the faith. For henceforth is laid up for me the crown of righteousness, which the Lord the righteous Judge shall give me at this day, and not to me only, but unto all them also which love his appearing," (2 Timothy 4:7-8). "For whosoever will save his life shall lose it; and whosoever shall lose his life for my sake, the same shall save it," (Luke 9:24). "Confirming the disciples hearts, and exhorting them to continue in the faith, affirming that we must through many afflictions enter into the kingdom of God," (Acts 14:22). "I John, even your brother and companion in tribulation, and in the kingdom and patience of Jesus Christ, was in the isle called Patmos, for the word of God, and for the witnessing of Jesus Christ," (Revelation 1:9). "But they overcame him by the blood of the Lamb, and by the word of their testimony, and they loved not their lives unto the death," (Revelation 12:11). "For we wrestle not against flesh and blood, but against principalities, against powers, and against the worldly governors, the princes of the darkness of this world," (Ephesians 6:12).

Now the Lord would have his Church so exposed to crosses, both for his own sake, and for hers, and for his enemies' sake: 1. For his own sake, that he might show his hatred of sin, even in his own, and the glory also of his power and mercy in their deliverance, as well as his justice in their afflictions. 2. For their sakes, that being in the warfare humbled and tamed for their sins, they might not perish with the world, (1 Corinthians 11:31-32) and may be herein like to Christ, (Romans 8:27). 3. For their enemies' sake, that they may know that they shall never be spared, if God does not spare his own children, "For the time is come that judgment must begin at the house of God: if it first begin at us, what shall the end be of them, which obey not the Gospel of God?" (1 Peter 4:17).

7. Seventhly, that she is invincible, "And I say also unto thee, that thou art Peter, and upon this rock I will build my Church; and the gates of hell shall not overcome it," (Matthew 16:18). "Nevertheless in all these things we are more than conquerors, through him that loved us. For I am persuaded that neither death, nor life, nor angels, nor principalities, nor powers, nor things present, nor things to come: Nor height, nor depth, nor any other creature shall be able to separate us from the love of God, which is in Christ Jesus our Lord," (Romans 8:37-39). "And the God of all grace, which hath called us unto his eternal glory by Christ Jesus, after that ye have suffered a little, make you perfect, confirm, strengthen, and stablish you," (1 Peter 5:10).

The uses of these principles may be either for instruction or consolation.

1. For instruction, and so the sound consideration of this may serve:

1. First, to stir us up to pray, that God would open our eyes to see the glory of his power and grace in the calling of his Church out of the world; and the most happy supremacy of Christ over the Church, and our own felicity, if we are members of the Church, (Ephesians 1:17).

2. Secondly, to enflame in us the care to make our calling and election sure, so that we may be infallibly assured that we

are members of the true church. If any ask for some plain sign, by which briefly the heart of man may establish itself in this point: I answer, that to be assured that we are true members of the church, and body of Christ, we must carefully try ourselves by such signs as these. For they are members of the church:

1. That are called out of the world by the voice of the preacher who cries out, and they are separated by the power of the word.

2. That rely on Christ's merits for righteousness and salvation.

3. That cleave to such as fear God with unchangeable affections, as the only people of the world.

4. That are reformed from their old evil conversation, to the constant endeavors of a holy life.

3. Thirdly, if we find ourselves to be of the church, we should strive for exceeding thankfulness to God, that has called us out of darkness to this marvelous light, and saved us from the common condemnation of the world, (1 Peter 2:9).

4. Fourthly, we should labor by holiness of life to exceed all the papists, or pagans of the world, that men might see by our piety, that God has done more for us than for any such as they. Our works should speak for us, that we are of the true church; and not by our sinful lives dishonor God, as our Father, or the church as our mother, (Ephesians 1:4, 2:8). Christ comes into his garden to see how his plants grow, "I went down to the garden of nuts, to see the fruits of the valley, to see if the vine budded, and if the pomegranates flourished," (Song of Solomon 6:10).

5. Fifthly, we should know no man after the flesh, nor reckon of men by their means in the world, but by their relation to Christ, or the church, "Wherefore henceforth know we no man after the flesh; yea though we have known Christ after the

flesh, yet now henceforth know we him no more," (2 Corinthians 5:16).

6. Sixthly, we should therefore avoid the society of the wicked, and not forsake the fellowship of the godly, "What concord hath Christ with Belial? or what part hath the believer with the infidel," (2 Corinthians 6:15). "Be not therefore companions with them," (Ephesians 5:7). "And have no fellowship with the unfruitful works of darkness, but even reprove them rather," (Ephesians 5:11). "If any man obey not our saying, note him by a letter, and have no company with him, that he may be ashamed," (2 Thessalonians 3:14). "Not forsaking the fellowship that we have among ourselves, as the manner of some is: but let us exhort one another, and that so much more, because ye see the day draweth near," (Hebrews 10:25).

7. Seventhly, we should therefore carry ourselves one towards another, as fellow-servants in the same family, and fellow-citizens in the same city, with all meekness, patience, unity, and love, "With all humbleness of mind, and meekness, with longsuffering, supporting one another through love, endeavoring to keep the unity of the spirit in the bond of peace," (Ephesians 4:2-3). Willingly employing our gifts for the good of the church, (Romans 12:6-8).

8. Eighthly, seeing we are in a continual warfare, we should stand on our guard, quitting us like men, and be strong, putting on all the armor of God, (Ephesians 6:10).

9. Ninthly, we should forever learn to think and speak reverently of the church of God, seeing it is the house of God, the family of Christ, the ground and pillar of truth, and that God's people are God's hidden ones, (Ephesians 3:15, 1 Timothy 3:15, Psalm 83:3). And in particular, both ministers and magistrates that are deputed to the government of the church

under Christ, should be careful to do their duties with all care. Ministers are charged in these Scriptures, (John 21:15-16, 1 Corinthians 12:18, 1 Timothy 3:15 as before).

And magistrates must remember that God has given them to be nursing fathers to the church, (Isaiah 60:10-11, 2 Chronicles 34:33, 35:3).

And here is matter of singular consolation for all the true members of the true church, if they consider:

First, the love of Christ toward them. He affecting them as a spouse or wife. (2 Corinthians 11:2, Revelation 19:7).

Secondly, the fellowship they have with Christ, "God is faithful, by whom ye are called into the fellowship of his Son Jesus Christ our Lord," (1 Corinthians 1:9).

Thirdly, the care of Christ for their sanctification, "Christ loved the church, and gave himself for it, that he might sanctify it, and cleanse it by the washing of water through the word," (Ephesians 5:25-26).

Fourthly, the royal furniture, with the which from Christ they are clad, being not destitute of any heavenly gifts, "So ye are not destitute of any gift, waiting for the appearing of our Lord Jesus Christ," (1 Corinthians 1:7). "Blessed be God, even the Father of our Lord Jesus Christ, which hath blessed us with all spiritual blessing in heavenly things in Christ," (Ephesians 1:3). "All the body furnished and knit together by joints and hands, increaseth with the increasing of God," (Colossians 2:19).

Fifthly, their safety in all their warfare, and their conquest and deliverance out of all their troubles, and their assurance of full happiness in the end. "Nevertheless in all these things we are more than conquerors through him that loved us: For I am persuaded that neither life nor death...Shall be able to separate us from the love of God, which is in Christ Jesus our

Lord," (Romans 8:37-39). "And he is the Head of the body of the church: he is the beginning, and the firstborn of the dead, that in all things he might have the preeminence," (Colossians 1:18). "The God of all grace, which hath called us unto his eternal glory by Christ Jesus, after that ye have suffered a little, will make you perfect, confirm, strengthen, and stablish you," (1 Peter 5:10).

And all this should comfort us more:

1. If we remember what we were, and are in ourselves. The church is black, (Song of Solomon 1:4). And the daughter of Pharaoh, (Psalm 45) and Christ found her out first in her blood, (Ezekiel 16:6).

2. If we consider that there is no respecting of persons with God; but the Eunuchs and the strangers may be admitted into the church, as well as the children of the kingdom, "Let not the son of the stranger which is joined to the Lord, speak, and say, the Lord hath surely separate me from his people, neither let the eunuch say, behold, I am a dry tree," (Isaiah 56:3).

CHAPTER 24:
Of Justification

We have covered the subject of grace, *viz.* the church: the degrees of grace in this life are two: First, justification. Secondly, sanctification.

1. Concerning justification, there are these principles:

1. First, that all men have sinned and the whole world is guilty before God naturally, and in themselves, "Now we know that whatsoever the law saith, it saith to them which are under the law; that every mouth may be stopped, and all the world be culpable before God. For there is no difference: for all have sinned and are deprived of the glory of God," (Romans 3:19,23). "But the Scripture hath concluded all under sin, that the promise by the faith of Jesus Christ should be given to them that believe," (Galatians 3:22).

2. Secondly, that by men's own works no flesh can be justified, "Therefore by the works of the law shall no flesh be justified in his sight: for by the law cometh the knowledge of sin," (Romans 3:20). "Not by the works of righteousness which we had done, but according to his mercy he saved us by the washing of the new birth, and the renewing of the Holy Ghost," (Titus 3:5). "And that no man is justified by the law in the sight of God, it is evident: for the just shall live by faith," (Galatians 3:11). "And might be found in him, that is, not having mine own righteousness, which is of the law, but that which is through the faith of Christ, even the righteousness, which is of God through faith," (Philippians 3:9).

Justified, I say, before God: for by works we may be justified before men, of which justification the Apostle James speaks in his second chapter.

3. Thirdly, that the righteousness which makes us just, is in Jesus Christ, being made ours by imputation. "For he hath made him to be sin for us, which knew no sin, that we should be made the righteousness of God in him," (2 Corinthians 5:21). "But ye are of him in Christ Jesus, who of God is made unto us wisdom, and righteousness, and sanctification, and redemption," (1 Corinthians 1:30). "Likewise then as by the offense of one, the fault came on all men to condemnation: so by the justifying of one, the benefit abounded toward all men to the justification of life: For as by one man's disobedience many were made sinners: so by the obedience of one, shall many also be made righteous," (Romans 5:18-19). "And might be found in him, that is, not having mine own righteousness, which is of the law, but that which is through the faith of Christ, even the righteousness which is of God through faith," (Philippians 3:9). "In his days Judah shall be saved, and Israel shall dwell safely, and this is the name, whereby they shall call him, The Lord our Righteousness," (Jeremiah 23:6). "Blessed are they, whose iniquities are forgiven, and whose sins are covered," (Romans 4:7).

4. That this righteousness is made ours only by faith, as it apprehends, and lays hold on, and relies on the righteousness of Christ, "Therefore we conclude that a man is justified by faith, without the works of the law," (Romans 3:28). "Know that a man is not justified by the works of the law, but by the faith of Jesus Christ, even we, I say, have believed in Jesus Christ, and not by the works of the law; because that by the works of the law no flesh shall be justified," (Galatians 2:16). "For I am not ashamed of the Gospel of Christ: for it is the power of God unto salvation to everyone that believeth; to the Jew first, and also to the Grecian: For by it the righteousness of God is revealed from faith to faith, as it is written: The just shall

live by faith," (Romans 1:16-17). "But without faith it is impossible to please God," (Hebrews 11:6).

5. That this faith is the gift of God, "Jesus answered and said unto them; This is the work of God, that ye believe in him, whom he hath sent," (John 6:29). "For I say through the grace that is given unto me, to everyone that is among you, that no man presume to understand: but that he understand according to sobriety, as God hath dealt to every man the measure of faith," (Romans 12:3). "For unto you it is given for Christ, that not only ye should believe in him, but also suffer for his sake," (Philippians 1:29). "For by grace are ye saved through faith, and that not of yourselves: it is the gift of God," (Ephesians 2:8). "Looking unto Jesus, the author and finisher of our faith," (Hebrews 12:2).

6. Sixthly, that all men do not have faith, "Who will believe our report? And to whom is the arm of the Lord revealed?" (Isaiah 53:1). "For all men have not faith," (2 Thessalonians 3:2).

And therefore this faith is called the faith of God's elect, "Paul, a servant of God, and an Apostle of Jesus Christ, according to the faith of God's elect," (Titus 1:1).

7. Seventhly, that there is but one kind of faith, by which all the elect are justified, "There is one Lord, one faith, one baptism," (Ephesians 4:5).

8. Eighthly, that being justified by faith, we have peace with God, and forgiveness of all our sins, "Whom God hath set forth to be a reconciliation through faith in his blood, to declare his righteousness by the forgiveness of sins, that are passed through the patience of God," (Romans 3:25). "Then being justified by faith, we have peace toward God through our Lord Jesus Christ," (Romans 5:1).

The consideration of these principles should work in us:

1. First, a special care of diverse duties: as,

1. The detestation of that doctrine that teaches men to rest upon merits of their own works, contrary to these express Scriptures, "Therefore by the works of the law shall no flesh be justified in his sight: for by the law cometh the knowledge of sin," (Romans 3:20). "For as many as are of the works of the law, are under the curse: for it is written, cursed is every man, that continueth not in all things, which are written in the book of the law to do them. "For by grace are ye saved through faith, and that not of yourselves, it is the gift of God: Not of works, lest any man should boast himself," (Ephesians 2:8-9). "Not by the works of righteousness which we had done, but according to his mercy he saved us," (Titus 3:5). All this we should carry in our minds.

2. The inflammation of the love of Christ in us, and the admiration of the riches of God's grace, "For Christ, when we were yet of no strength, at this time died for the ungodly. Doubtless one will scarce die for a righteous man: but yet for a good man it may be, that one dare die. But God setteth out his love toward us, seeing that while we were yet sinners, Christ died for us," (Romans 5:6-8).

3. A special care above all things to believe, accounting all things but dung, in comparison of the knowledge of Christ here. Without this faith it is impossible to please God, (Hebrews 11:6). We should never rest, until we could say, it is the Lord our righteousness, (Jeremiah 23:6). We are undone, if we do not have such a faith as will justify us.

Question: Tell us distinctly, what we must do about believing, which being done, we may be sure we are justified?

Solution: First, you must believe that Jesus of Nazareth is the promised Messiah, and the very Son of God, (Matthew 16:16). "Whosoever confesseth that Jesus is the Son of God, in him dwelleth God, and he is in God," (1 John 4:15).

Secondly, you must rest on the passion and obedience of Jesus Christ, as the only sufficient means of your happiness, receiving the promises, that declare your liberty so to do, (Romans 4:23-24, Romans 5:17).

Thirdly, you must in your prayers present Christ to God, and make it known as a covenant of your heart, that you rely on him only; and so give glory to God against the fear of the law, sin, death and hell.

Fourthly, you must resolve to rest in this course, and never to depart from your confidence in this. The just must live by their faith. So we have considered this third use.

4. Fourthly, we should be stirred up to show forth daily the use and power and truth of our justification by the effects of it; which we should strive to stir up in us, as namely we should show that we are justified:

1. By confirming our consciences in peace and tranquility.

2. By going boldly to God, and the throne of his grace; as knowing in how much grace we stand with God.

3. By comforting ourselves in hope of glory, knowing that we are heirs of Christ and the whole world.

4. By glorying in tribulation, being never ashamed of our faith and hope, (Romans 5:1-5).

5. The doctrine of our free justification should teach us to carry ourselves with all compassion and meekness toward other men, that yet live in their sins: for we were such as they once, till the grace of God appeared without and desert of ours.

Put them in remembrance, that they be "subject to the principalities, and powers, and that they be obedient and ready to every good work. That they speak evil of no man; that they be no fighters, but soft, showing all meekness unto all men: For we ourselves were in times past unwise, disobedient, deceived, serving the lusts and diverse pleasures, living in maliciousness, and envy, hateful, and hating one another."

6. We should be careful of good works, to free the glorious doctrine of liberty from the aspersions of evil men, and to show our thankfulness to God, and the truth of our faith, "Do we then make the law of none effect through faith? God forbid; yea we establish the law," (Romans 3:31, James 2, the latter part of the chapter). "That we being justified by his grace, should not be made heirs according to the hope of eternal life. This is a true saying, and these things I will thou shouldest affirm, that they which have believed in God, might be careful to show forth good works," (Titus 3:7-8).

7. This should make us forever to judge of men's worth by their faith, and to say, Oh, he, or she is blessed, that believed;[13] and to account highly of poor Christians, that are rich in faith.

8. Forever while we live, we should not glory in ourselves, but in the Lord, acknowledging whatsoever we are, we are by the grace of God, "That according as it is written, He that rejoiceth, let him rejoice in the Lord," (1 Corinthians 1:31). "Where is then the rejoicing? It is excluded: by what law? of works: Nay, but by the law of faith," (Romans 3:27).

Secondly, this doctrine should work in us much consolation, even from the dead: Justification is called

---

[13] James 2:5.

justification of life, (Romans 5:18). It should quicken us above many other doctrines, and the rather if we consider,

1. That in Christ there is a daily propitiation for all our sins, (Romans 3:25, 1 John 2:2). He will see our filthy garments taken off us, and clothe us with change of raiment, (Zechariah 3:3-4).

2. That the very blessing of Abraham comes on us; we are heirs of the world as well as he is, "They which be of faith, are blessed with faithful Abraham," (Galatians 3:9, Romans 4:11-12).

3. That though this is clogged with a condition of believing; yet we are not excepted, but may lawfully rest upon Christ; yea we are commanded to believe, "This is then his commandment, that we believe in the name of his Son Jesus Christ," (1 John 3:23). Yes, God beseeches us to be reconciled, "Now then are we ambassadors for Christ, as though God did beseech you through us, we pray you in Christ's stead, that ye be reconciled to God," (2 Corinthians 5:20).

4. That this believing in Christ makes us accounted as righteous as ever Adam was, or we could have been, if we had kept the moral law, and God is as well pleased with us: our faith is accounted for righteousness, and instead of it, "But to him that worketh not, but believeth him that justifieth the ungodly, his faith is counted for righteousness," (Romans 4:5).

5. That we may from here gather also assurance of reigning with God in another world, as the Apostle shows, "Much more than being now justified by his blood, we shall be saved from wrath through him. For if when we were enemies, we were reconciled to God by the death of his Son; much more being reconciled, we shall be saved by his life," (Romans 5:9-11). "For if by the offense of one death reigned through one; much more shall they which receive the abundance of grace,

and the gift of righteousness reign in life through one, that is, Jesus Christ," (Romans 5:17). "Whom he justified, them he also glorified," (Romans 8:30).

6. Lastly, that nothing shall separate us from this love of God, no accusation shall be received against us, (Romans 8:33-34).

Thirdly, this may serve for great reproof,

1. First, for the neglect of faith in many; O who has bewitched you, that you should not believe? Why will you still be shut up, and live under the curse? "O foolish Galatians, who hath bewitched you," (Galatians 3:1). "As many as are under the works of the law, are under the curse," (Galatians 3:10). "Before faith came, we were kept under the law, and shut up," (Galatians 3:23).

2. Of the most of us, for leaning still too much to our own works; we can hardly tell how in our either glorying, or grieving, to quit ourselves from the infection of pleading a merit of works.

3. Of many dear servants of God for their slothfulness and miserable neglect of the assurance of faith; resting still in their weakness of faith, and not striving to be fully persuaded.

CHAPTER 25:
Of Sanctification

"For this is the will of God, even your sanctification," (1 Thessalonians 4:4).

We have considered justification; sanctification follows. Concerning sanctification there are these principles:

1. That whom God justifies, he sanctifies, "Moreover whom he predestined, them also he called, and whom he called, them also he justified, and whom he justified, them he also glorified," (Romans 8:30). "A new heart also will I give you and a new Spirit will I put within you, and I will take away the stony heart out of your body, and I will give you an heart of flesh. And I will put my Spirit within you, and cause you to walk in my statutes, and ye shall keep my judgments and do them," (Ezekiel 36:26-27).

2. That to be truly sanctified, is to die to sin, and to rise again to newness of life, "What shall we say then? Shall we continue in sin, that grace may abound? God forbid: how shall we that are dead to sin, live yet therein? Know ye not that all we which have been baptized into Jesus Christ, have been baptized into his death? We are buried then with him by baptism into his death, that like as Christ was raised up from the dead by the glory of the Father, so we also should walk in newness of life," (Romans 6:1-4). Or it is to repent and believe the Gospel, "The time is fulfilled, and the kingdom of God is at hand: repent, and believe the Gospel," (Mark 1:15).

3. That except we are born again, we cannot enter into the kingdom of God, "Jesus answered, verily, verily, I say unto thee, except that a man be born of water and of the Spirit, he

cannot enter into the kingdom of God," (John 3:5). "Follow peace with all men, and holiness, without the which no man shall see the Lord," (Hebrews 12:14). "But if we walk in the light, as he is in the light, we have fellowship one with another, and the blood of Jesus Christ his Son cleanseth us from all sin," (1 John 1:7). "Therefore if any man be in Christ, let him be a new creature: old things are passed away, behold all things are become new," (2 Corinthians 5:17).

4. Fourthly, that sanctification is God's gift, and work in Jesus Christ; we can no more convert ourselves, than we can beget ourselves at first. We can no more create ourselves new men, than we can create ourselves men, "Him hath God lifted up with his right hand to be a Prince, and a Savior, to give repentance to Israel, and forgiveness of sins," (Acts 5:31). "When they heard these things, they held their peace, and glorified God saying: then hath God also to the Gentiles granted repentance unto life," (Acts 11:18). "Instructing them with meekness, that are contrary minded; proving if God at any time will give them repentance, that they may know the truth," (2 Timothy 2:25). "But ye are of him in Christ Jesus, who of God is made unto us wisdom, and righteousness, and sanctification and redemption," (1 Corinthians 1:30). "Thus the heathen shall know that I the Lord do sanctify Israel, when my sanctuary shall be amongst them forevermore," (Ezekiel 37:28). "Not by the works of righteousness which we had done, but according to his mercy he saved us by the washing of the new birth, and the renewing of the Holy Ghost," (Titus 3:5).

5. Fifthly, that our sanctification is imperfect while we live in this world, "If we say that we have no sin, we deceive ourselves, and the truth is not in us," (1 John 1:8). "For a just man falleth seven times and riseth again: but the wicked fall into mischief," (Proverbs 24:16). "But we have all been as an

unclean thing, and all our righteousness is as filthy clouts; and we do all fade like a leaf, and our iniquities like the wind have taken us away," (Isaiah 64:6).

The uses may be for information, instruction, humiliation, and consolation.

1. For the first, we may here take notice of the wisdom of God in curing the posterity of Adam. We receive double disease from Adam: the one was the guilt of eternal death: the other was corruption of nature. By justification the first was abolished, and by sanctification the other is healed by degrees.

2. For the second, we may here learn many things:

1. The first is carefully to study our own sanctification, and compel on ourselves a more constant endeavor of sound reformation. To this end I propound two things:

1. Certain motives which we should have continually in our minds, to stir up to the care of holiness, and to get true grace.

2. Certain rules, which may exceedingly further us about our sanctification.

The motives are these, among many:

1. The commandment of God, "This is the will of God, even your sanctification," (1 Thessalonians 4:3). "For we are his workmanship, created in Christ Jesus unto good works, which God hath ordained that we should walk in them," (Ephesians 2:10).

2. The conscience of our debt, which we owe herein, "Therefore brethren we are debtors, not to the flesh to live after the flesh," (Romans 8:12) being redeemed by Christ. "Who gave himself for us, that he might redeem us from all iniquity, and purge us to be a peculiar people to himself, zealous of good works," (Titus 2:14).

3. The consideration of our own dignity: we are the children of God, the temples of the Holy Ghost, kings and priests unto God; God's own peculiar people and inheritance.

4. The rich promises that belong to godliness, "For bodily exercise profiteth little: but godliness is profitable unto all things, which hath the promise of the life present, and of that that is to come," (1 Timothy 4:8).

5. The assurance of this in our calling and election, "Wherefore brethren, give rather diligence to make your calling and election sure: for it ye do these things, ye shall never fall," (2 Peter 1:10).

6. The excellency of good works: they are sacrifices seasoned with the salt of faith, kindled with the fire of the Holy Spirit, offered by the merit of Christ, and accepted of God, "And ye be made a holy priesthood, to offer up spiritual sacrifices acceptable to God by Jesus Christ," (1 Peter 2:5).

7. The silencing of the ignorant from speaking evil, "For so is the will of God, that by well doing ye may put to silence the ignorance of the foolish," (1 Peter 2:15).

8. Because otherwise,

1. The name of God will be blasphemed, "For the name of God is blasphemed among the Gentiles, through you," (Romans 2:24). "Howbeit because by this deed thou hast caused the enemies of the Lord to blaspheme, the child that is born unto thee shall surely die," (2 Samuel 12:14).

2. The Spirit of God will be grieved, and the works of the Spirit deadened, "And grieve not the Holy Spirit of God, by whom ye are sealed unto the day of redemption," (Ephesians 4:30).

3. The judgment of God will be provoked, (Psalm 89:31-32).

The rules we need to be put in mind of, that concern sanctification, either show us what to take heed of, or what to do.

That we are not deceived in this great work of true grace, we must take heed,

1. First, of wretchlessness and security, by which a man lives so, as he is insensible and careless of reformation altogether. "Awake thou that sleepest," (Ephesians 5:14).

2. Secondly, of the daily baits, and methods of sin. Do not be "ensnared with the pleasures of sin, which are but for a season; but circumcise betimes the foreskins of your hearts," (Jeremiah 4:4).

3. Thirdly, of procrastination, and delaying of time in the business of reformation. For your life is uncertain, (Matthew 25:13) and every day adds to the heap of sin, and of wrath, (Romans 2:5). Do not sin against your purposes of amendment, lest your grow more hardened.

4. Fourthly, of hypocrisy, and pretended holiness, (Isaiah 58:2, Lamentations 4:8).

5. Fifthly, of the persuasion of the merit of your own works, "For they being ignorant of the righteousness of God, and going about to stablish their own righteousness, have not submitted themselves to the righteousness of God," (Romans 10:3).

6. Of temporary righteousness, "Ephraim, what shall I do unto thee? O Judah, how shall I entreat thee? For your goodness is as a morning cloud, and as a morning dew it goeth away," (Hosea 6:4). Or being weary of well doing, "Let us not therefore be weary of well doing: for in due season we shall reap, if we faint not," (Galatians 6:9).

7. Seventhly, of the precepts of men, "In vain they worship me, teaching for doctrine man's precepts," (Matthew

15:9). "But I said unto their children in the wilderness, walk ye not in the ordinances of your fathers, neither observe their manners, nor defile yourselves with their idols," (Ezekiel 20:18).

8. Eighthly, of looking after the example, and fashion of the world, "Frame not yourselves like unto this world," (Romans 12:2).

9. Ninthly, neglect of prayer for the particular furtherance of reformation and grace, (Lamentations 5:21) shall he not give us his Holy Spirit, if we ask him, as our Savior shows in the parable.

10. Tenthly, let the best of us take heed of a strange deceit, and that is to rest in fair words, and attentive hearing. How is it that men that hear many precious counsels, comforts, and reproofs, go away without any reformation, and think they do well, if they commend the sermon? O, how common is this disease, or medicine, and they fall asleep before it is applied like those hearers in the Gospel, of whom it is said, "They heard, they marveled, and they went their ways."

So we have considered what we should avoid, that the work of sanctification is not hindered.

On the other hand there are diverse things to be observed by us, as,

1. First, we must look to the matter to be done, which has two considerations in it:

1. That in general whatever things are true, honest, just, pure, lovely, and of good report, that have virtue and praise in them, that we should think on those things, and study how to glorify God, and enrich ourselves by well doing them, (Philippians 4:8, Ephesians 5:8).

2. That we strive to keep ourselves free from, or speedily mortify such evils as usually stain the profession of religion

after calling. Besides the mortification of gross evils, which the first repentance puts away; we must watch carefully against other sins, such as are lying, rotten communication, deceit, anger, wrath, and all bitterness, and cursed speaking, (Colossians 3:8, Ephesians 4:25).

2. Secondly, we must look to the end of all our actions, the end I say both of intention, and continuance: For

1. We must propound the glory of God, as the main end of all our actions, "Whether therefore ye eat or drink, or whatsoever ye do, do all to the glory of God," (1 Corinthians 10:31, Philippians 1:11).

2. We must so begin to reformation and good works, as we are sure also to endeavor with all constancy to hold out to the end, "All the days of our life in holiness and righteousness before him. "Blessed are they that keep judgment, and do righteousness at all times," (Psalm 106:3).

3. Thirdly, we must look to the manner of our reformation, that it be done with all sincerity, and so we do,

1. If we turn from all sorts of our transgressions, "Therefore I will judge you, O house of Israel, every one according to his ways; return therefore, and cause others to turn away from all your transgressions, so iniquity shall not be your destruction. Cast away from you all your transgressions, whereby ye have transgressions, and make you a new heart, and a new Spirit: for why will ye die, O house of Israel?" (Ezekiel 18:30-31).

2. If we labor for a sanctification that is throughout in all parts, in soul, in body, and in spirit, that is, in our outward man, and in our affections, and in our judgments, and thoughts.

4. Fourthly, we must be exceedingly mindful of the means of sanctification, and so we must especially think of,

1. The Word, to subject ourselves to its power; for if "we hear our souls shall live," we are "sanctified by the truth," and God will have "his law magnified," and "the Word is able to build us up still further," till we come to heaven, (Isaiah 55:4, John 17:19, Isaiah 42:21, Acts 20:32).

2. The Sabbath: for that is the sign of our sanctification. It is a sign to assure, that God will not fail us in his blessings; and it is a sign that we are indeed a holy people, if we be careful to keep the Sabbath. It is the market day for our souls, and by the right keeping of the Sabbath, we shall be the better able to serve God all the week after, "Keep ye my Sabbaths: for it is a sign between me and you in your generation, that ye may know, that I the Lord do sanctify you. Ye shall therefore keep the Sabbath, for it is holy unto you; he that defileth it shall die the death; therefore whosoever worketh therein, the same person shall be even cut off from among his people," (Exodus 31:13-14). "Blessed is the man that doth this, and the son of man which layeth hold on it: he that keepeth the Sabbath, and polluteth it not, and keepeth his hand from doing any evil," (Isaiah 56:2). So much for the uses for instruction.

3. Thirdly, these principles may terrify all men that are unsanctified, that do not have true grace, that live in their sins. Woe to world of men because of sin! For thereby they may gather, that there is no cure done to their natures, that they do not all become justified before God, that they have no part with Christ, and that all they do is still impure, (Matthew 7:18, Titus 1:15). Yes, and that the wages of their sins will be death, and that in the state they are in, they cannot be saved, (Romans 6:23, John 3:5) and in the meantime, what do they know, and how can they tell how soon the whirlwind of the Lord may fall on the wicked? "Behold, the tempest of the Lord goeth forth in

his wrath and a violent whirlwind shall fall down upon the head of the wicked," (Jeremiah 23:19).

And for all the things they have done in the flesh, they must come to judgment; and the rather because they have not taken warnings, "Because he hath appointed a day in which he will judge the world in righteousness by that man, whom he hath appointed," (Acts 17:31).

Objection: But someone may say, what do you tell of these terrible things? We have no reason to think of ourselves, that we are unsanctified, how can we, or you tell, who are not sanctified?

Solution: It is easy to tell in the negative, who are not sanctified, you may know it of wicked men:

1. Because they are asleep, and dead in sin, and do not have any true feeling of the hatefulness of their many sins, "And you hath he quickened, that were dead in trespasses and sins," (Ephesians 2:1).

2. Because sin reigns in them, it has an unlimited power in them, "Let not sin reign therefore in your mortal body, that ye should obey it in the lusts thereof."

3. Because they sin by covenant, they hire themselves; their purpose is with their whole hearts to commit and continue in sin, they obey as servants, "Know ye not that to whomsoever ye give yourselves, as servants to obey, his servants ye are to whom ye obey, whether it be of sin unto death, or of obedience unto righteousness," (Romans 6:16).

4. Because they are silent from prayer, and confession of sin, (Psalm 32:23,5).

5. Because they have no favor of the things of the Spirit but altogether favor fleshly things, "For they that are after the flesh, savor the things of the flesh: but they that are after the Spirit, the things of the Spirit," (Romans 8:5).

6. Because they never had any marriage affections to Jesus Christ, (Romans 7:5).

7. Lastly, a wicked man finds in himself not only an impotency, but an impossibility to be subject to the law of God. He resolves that he cannot possibly yield to the directions of the word, nor will not: where a godly mind loves the law, desires to obey, endeavors it, subjects himself to it, though he fails and sins in many ways.

4. Fourthly and lastly, the godly may be comforted in the observation of this work of the Spirit of grace, that is in Jesus Christ, which kills sin in them, and has made them alive from the dead.

Objection. But some weak Christian might say, there is much comfort in this doctrine of the healing of their natures, except that the imperfection of their sanctification is a continual discomfort.

Solution. Christians may and ought to comfort themselves against the imperfection of their sanctification many ways, and so if they look,

1. Upon the Spirit of God in their hearts, and so two things may relieve; first the assistance of the Spirit, which will help their infirmities, (Romans 8:26). And then if they consider the very fountain of all good actions, and every good gift to be the same Spirit of God, they must needs conclude it is some divine thing which is wrought in them, inasmuch as it flows from the Holy Spirit; however it is imperfect through the corruption of their hearts.

2. Upon Jesus Christ; and so if they behold,

1. His intercession, and that likewise has a double comfort in it. For, first Christ made intercession for us, when he prayed for our sanctification, it should much comfort us to remember that our sanctification was one of the things Christ

prayed for, (John 17:19). Secondly, Christ in his intercession in heaven, covers all the imperfections of the godly, and is their advocate before the Father, (1 John 2:2, Romans 8:34).

2. His death and resurrection, from where flows a virtue continually, which is of singular power, to make our sins still die in us, and quicken us to newness of life, (Romans 6:4). For this cause Christ sanctified himself, that he might sanctify his members by the influence from him, as from their head, (John 17:17).

3. Upon the hope of perfect holiness: for the time will come, when they shall be without spot or wrinkle, (Ephesians 5:27). The merit of their perfect holiness is found in the price paid by Jesus Christ, (Hebrews 10:14). It should much solace them, that one day their shall be a perpetual end of all sin and infirmities.

4. If in the meantime they look on the good nature of God, assuring them by his promises,

1. That they are under grace, and not under the law, (Romans 6:14).

2. That he will not deal with us after our sins, (Psalm 103).

3. That he will spare us, as a man spares his son that serves him, (Malachi 3:17).

4. That he will accept of the will and desire for the deed, (2 Corinthians 8:12).

5. That he is slow to anger, and ready to forgive, (Psalm 103:8). And mercy pleases him, (Micah 7:18).

6. That he will pass by our infirmities and mere frailties, and not take notice of them, (Micah 7:18).

CHAPTER 26:
Of the Resurrection

"Marvel not at this: for the hour shall come, in the which all that are in the graves, shall hear his voice: And they shall come forth that have done good, unto the resurrection of life; but they that have done evil, upon the resurrection of condemnation," (John 5:28-29).

We have covered the principles that concern the third estate of man. The fourth estate of man is the estate of glory; and in this we are to consider the three degrees of it:

1. The resurrection of the body.
2. The last judgment.
3. The glory of heaven.

The principles concerning the resurrection are these:

First, that the bodies of dead men shall rise out of the dust of the earth, and their own souls shall enter into them again, "For I am sure that my Redeemer liveth, and he shall stand at the latter day upon the earth. And though after my skin worms destroy this body, yet shall I see God in my flesh," (Job 19:23,26). "Thy dead men shall live; even with my body shall they rise: Awake and sing ye that dwell in dust: for thy dew is as the dew of herbs, and the earth shall cast out the dead," (Isaiah 26:19). "Marvel not at this, for the hour shall come, in the which all that are in the graves, shall hear his voice," (John 5:28). "For if the dead be not raised, then is Christ not raised," (1 Corinthians 15:16, *cf.* the whole chapter).

Secondly, the bodies of all men shall be raised, (John 5:28) as before. Small and great; the earth, sea, fire, beasts, fowls, air, and shall deliver up their dead, "And I saw the dead, both great and small, stand before God; and the books were opened, and another book was opened, which is the book of life, and the dead were judged of those things which were written in the books, according to their works. And the sea gave up here dead which were in her, and death and hell delivered up the dead which were in them, and they were judged every man according to their works," (Revelation 20:12-13). Just and unjust shall rise "And have hope toward God, that the resurrection of the dead, which they themselves look for also, shall be both of just and unjust," (Acts 24:15). "Though the unjust shall not rise in the same manner, nor by the same power, that is, by the virtue shall not rise in the same manner, nor by the same power, that is by the virtue of Christ's resurrection, "And many of them that sleep in the dust of the earth shall awake, some to everlasting life, and some to shame and perpetual contempt," (Daniel 12:2).

Question. It may be objected, that Daniel says many shall rise, not all.

Answer. He may speak so because we shall not die; but those that are alive at Christ's coming, shall be changed instead of death and resurrection, "For this say we unto you by the word of the Lord, that we which live, and are remaining in the coming of the Lord, shall not prevent them which sleep," (1 Thessalonians 4:15).

Thirdly, that the same bodies, which men carry about with them in this world shall rise again, "And though after my skin worms destroy this body, yet shall I see God in my flesh. Whom I myself shall see, and mine eyes shall behold, and none other for me, though my reins are consumed within me," (Job 19:26-27). "He keepeth all his bones, not one of them is broken, "Psalm 34:20).

This very corruptible must put on incorruption, "For this corruptible must put on incorruption, and this mortal must put on immortality," (1 Corinthians 15:53).

The reasons are, 1. Because every man shall receive in his body, what he has done, either good or evil, "For we must all appear before the judgment seat of Christ, that every man may receive the things which are done in his body, according to that he has done, whether good or evil," (2 Corinthians 5:10).

2. Because otherwise it would be absurd that any other body should be crowned, but that which suffered: or punished, but that which sinned.

Fourthly, that this resurrection shall be at the end of the world, even the last day of the world, "No man can come to me, except the Father which hath sent me draw him: and I will raise him up at the last day," (John 6:44).

And therefore, we must distinguish between particular resurrections and the general or universal. Particular resurrections have been past in some cases miraculously, as at the time of Christ's death: but the principle speaks of the universal resurrection.

The uses may be for information, instruction, consolation, and terror.

1. First, for information, and so we should strive to inform ourselves in three things:

1. The certainty of it, that it shall surely be.

2. The manner of it, since it must necessarily be.

3. The glory of the life in Christ, that can effect this.

1. For the first, we may find many ways to affect our hearts with a full assurance that our dead bodies shall rise again: many things tend to this, some probable, some infallible, some show it that it *may* be, others that it *shall* be.

That it is not impossible, other works in nature show: as first, the phoenix, a bird in Arabia, of which it is written that getting old, with the sticks of frankincense and cassia, with which she filled her nest, she makes a fire, and being put in the fire, and burned to ashes, by and by after the dew of heaven lights on her, she comes forth alive. Secondly, we know that many little birds, which for the wintertime lie out of the way in deep marshes, or such like places; yet in springtime come out alive again. Thirdly, we see that trees and plants in winter lose all their ornaments, and being dead for a time in sight, yet they are revived again. Fourthly, in this way does the seed also which the husbandman throws into the ground, "O fool, that which thou sowest is not quickened except it die," (1 Corinthians 15:36). Fifthly and lastly, night and day, sleep and waking, shows us this: the day dies into the night, and yet revives to the world with all his glory.

Yes, in man himself there is grounds of singular probability:

1. First, his deliverances from dangers and distresses, are (as it were) lesser resurrections, and the term is given to it. The houses in which the Jews were captives, were as so many graves; and their return, as a rising from the dead, (Ezekiel 37:12, 2 Corinthians 1:10).

2. Secondly, he has had an experience of the first resurrection in his soul already, and how can he doubt the rising of his body? (Romans 6, John 5:25,28, Revelation 20:6).

3. Thirdly, diverse particular men have appeared raised from the dead; as Lazarus, (John 13:43) the saints that appeared out of the graves after Christ's death, (Matthew 27:52-53).

4. Fourthly, God showed this in a vision to Ezekiel, when he saw a field full of dry bones, receiving at God's commandment flesh, and nerves, and life, (Ezekiel 37).

But we have more than probabilities, we have certain arguments for it, as

1. First, the word of God assuring it, (1 Thessalonians 4:15) as was proved before, to whom all things are possible, "For with God shall nothing be impossible," (Luke 1:37). "The things which are impossible with men, are possible with God," (Luke 18:27, Romans 4:21).

2. Secondly, the Son of God undertaking to effect it, "And this is the Father's will which he hath sent me, that of all which he hath given me, I should lose nothing, but should raise it up again at the last day," (John 6:39).

3. Thirdly, the resurrection of Christ to assure it, who rose as our surety, (1 Thessalonians 4:14).

4. Fourthly, the sacrament of baptism seals both the resurrection of the soul and body.

5. Fifthly and lastly, the Apostle proves at large the necessity of the resurrection, by many arguments: showing the Gospel is overturned, if the resurrection is not believed, (1 Corinthians 15:12).

So much for considering that it shall be. *How* it shall be, follows: The manner of the resurrection will be in this way:

1. First, when the last day of the world is come, Christ will come all of a sudden, in the same visible form he went to heaven, will come in the clouds with his angels and thousands of the souls of his saints, (Jude 14, 1 Thessalonians 4:15).

2. Secondly, the trumpet of God shall then sound, the voice of the Archangel shall then be heard. Christ shall command, exhort, and call upon the dead to rise and come away to judgment, (1 Thessalonians 4:16-17) so as the very dead shall hear this shout and voice of Christ, (John 5:29, Matthew 24:31).

3. Thirdly, immediately the spirit of Christ will bring the souls of all the godly, and they shall enter into their bodies; and then those that have slept in the dust of the earth, shall be raised to life.

4. Fourthly, the bodies of the wicked shall then be raised also by the power of God, by a way unknown.

5. Fifthly, men that shall then be alive, shall have a change all of a sudden instead of death, and resurrection, (1 Corinthians 15, 1 Thessalonians 4:15-16).

6. Sixthly, the angels shall then gather the elect, and chase in reprobates from the four winds of heaven, and present them before Christ, (Matthew 24:31). So much for the manner.

3. Thirdly, this may inform us concerning the glorious life of the Son of God, who does not only live himself; but gives life to millions of men by his Spirit, (John 5:21) and raised dead bodies so miraculously. We have considered the use for information.

From the doctrine of the resurrection we should learn diverse things.

1. First, it should teach us not to mourn immoderately for the dead, since when Christ comes again, he will bring them with him; and the earth and seas shall make a true account of their dead in the day of Christ, (1 Thessalonians 4:13-14).

2. Secondly, it should teach us to have our very bodies in honor, and not to transgress against it, seeing it is redeemed by Christ, and shall be raised to immortality at the last day.

Now men sin against the body in the following manner:

1. When (according to the traditions of men, and through will-worship) they withhold from the body due sustenance, (Colossians 2:23).

2. When men pollute their bodies, that should be prepared to immortality, with filthiness; such as is whoredom,

drunkenness, sodomy, and such like abominations, (1 Corinthians 6:13-14).

3. When the bodies of the saints are not carefully and with meet honor buried, or their burying places uncivilly disregarded.

3. Thirdly, the consideration of this great work of the resurrection of men's bodies should teach us to trust God in lesser matters, and believe his promises, though there be never so great unlikelihood of the accomplishment, in respect of outward means and appearance, (Romans 4:17-18).

4. Fourthly, we should especially be careful to get the assurance that our bodies shall have a glorious resurrection, (Acts 24:15). And that we may be so assured:

1. We must pray God to give us his Holy Spirit, as the pledge of it. For then if the Spirit of Christ is in us, the same Spirit that raised Christ, will raise up our natural bodies at the last day, (Romans 8:11).

2. We must be sure of the first resurrection, that the body be dead in respect of sin and the soul raised up to a lively care of newness of life: those that have their part in the first resurrection, shall never taste of the second death, (Romans 6, Revelation 20:6).

3. In particular, we must be sure to get faith in Jesus Christ, who is the resurrection, and the life, and in whom whosoever believes, he shall not die forever, (John 11:25).

5. Fifthly, we should resolve to live like such as believe a glorious resurrection, and to this end:

1. We should be steadfast, and immovable in all conditions of life, (1 Corinthians 15:58).

2. We should live as men devoted wholly to the service of Jesus Christ, whose we are both in life and death, (Romans 14:7-8).

3. We should strive to abound in the work of the Lord, (1 Corinthians 15:58) rousing up ourselves to the care of well doing, (1 Corinthians 15:34) studying to keep a conscience void of offense toward God and man, (Acts 24:16).

4. Our minds should run on that time considered as if we were in heaven, and our conversation should be in heaven, (Philippians 3:20). So, we have considered the uses for instruction.

Thirdly, the doctrine of the resurrection has singular comfort in it, and Christians are charged to comfort themselves, and one another with these things, (1 Thessalonians 4:18). And David rejoiced and was glad at heart for this reason, (Psalm 16:9). For that is the time of the refreshing of all Christians, (Acts 3:19). And so, the godly have been accustomed to comfort themselves against diverse maladies, as,

1. Against the pains and tortures of the body; so did Job, "For I am sure, that my Redeemer liveth, and he shall stand the last on earth. And though after my skin, worms destroy this body; yet shall I see God in my flesh. Whom I myself shall see, and mine eyes shall behold, and none other for me, though my reins are consumed within me," (Job 19:25-27).

And so did the godly mentioned, "The women received their dead raised to life; others also were racked, and would not be delivered, that they might receive a better resurrection," (Hebrews 11:35).

2. Against the troubles and general miseries of this life, and so God's people are comforted, "And at that time shall Michael stand up, the great prince which standeth for the children of thy people; and there shall be a time of trouble, such as was never since there began to be a nation unto the same time; and at that time thy people shall be delivered, every one

that shall be found written in the book. And many of them that sleep in the dust of the earth, shall awake, some to everlasting life, and some to shame and perpetual contempt," (Daniel 12:1-2). "Thy dead men shall live; even with my body shall they rise; Awake, and sing ye that dwell in dust; for thy dew is as the dew of herbs, and the earth shall cast out the dead," (Isaiah 26:19).

3. Against death itself and so the Apostle triumphs, "O death where is thy sting! O grave where is thy victory! The sting of death is sin: and the strength of sin is the law. But thanks be unto God, which hath given us victory through our Lord Jesus Christ," (1 Corinthians 15:55-57).

Objection: Now if any ask, what in the doctrine of the resurrection should comfort us in those cases?

Solution: I answer, the consideration of the marvelous glory of our bodies, in which they should rise, should fill us with sweet refreshings, "Who shall change our vile body, that it may be fashioned like unto his glorious body, according to the working whereby he is able to subdue all things unto himself," (Philippians 3:21). For six things shall befall our bodies in that day:

1. Immortality: so as they can never die again, (1 Corinthians 15:42-44,53).

2. Incorruption: they shall never be inclined to putrefaction or any other corruption.

3. Spiritualness: our bodies shall be raised spiritual bodies; they shall be like spirits, as it were, and that in diverse respects:

1. Because they shall be possessed fully by the Spirit of God, so as they shall be both governed by the Spirit, and be subject to the Spirit wholly.

2. Because they shall live as the angels in heaven do, without meat or raiment, or any other bodily helps or sustenance.

3. Because they shall be for nimbleness, as it were *spirits*, they shall be able with incredible swiftness to pass into all the parts of the world, earth, or air, for they shall meet "Christ in the air," (1 Thessalonians 4:17).

4. Power: for of bodies full of weakness, and subject to many calamities and distresses, and pains, they shall be raised in power; that is, strong, able, and impassable.

5. Perfection: for they shall be freed from deformity, unhandsomeness, maims, lameness, and become most fair and comely; neither infancy, nor old age hindering them, but shall appear in full age and beauty.

6. Shining and splendor, as the sun or stars in the firmament: the body being clothed with a celestial glory and divine light, "And they that be wise, shall shine as brightness of the firmament; and they shall turn many to righteousness, shall shine as the stars forever and ever," (1 Corinthians 15:40, Daniel 12:3). "Then shall the just men shine as the sun in the kingdom of their Father: He that has ears to hear, let him hear," (Matthew 13:43).

And as we may comfort ourselves by the mediation of these distinct glories in our bodies then, so it may add to our comfort, and the establishment of it, if we consider three things more; to wit, first, the certainty of all this, that it shall come. Secondly, the shortness of the time here. Thirdly, the condition of the body until then.

1. For the first, we should not doubt of it, because we are born again to this hope, we are children of the resurrection now, and so called, (Luke 20:36). And besides, Christ has a charge to lose nothing; no, not even of the bodies of the saints,

"And this is the Father's will, which hath sent me, that of all which he hath given me, I should lose nothing, but should raise it up again at the last day," (John 6:39).

And he came to this end, to dissolve the works of the devil, which is sin, and death by sin, (1 John 3:8). Christ also is the first fruits of the dead, (1 Corinthians 15:20). And further we have felt the power of Christ in raising our souls already: he that by his word made all things, can by the same voice bring back our bodies again.

Objection: That the bodies resolved to dust and ashes, should rise, is against common sense and reason.

Solution: It is above reason, but not against it. Can men of ashes make glass, and cannot God of dust make the body again?

Objection: But the dead bodies are often mingled with the bodies of beasts or other creatures.

Solution: The goldsmith by his art can sever metals, and extract one metal out of another, and can God not distinguish these dusts?

Objection: Flesh and blood cannot come into the kingdom of heaven, (1 Corinthians 15:50).

Solution: By flesh and blood is not meant the body simply, but as it is clothed with sin and infirmity, which shall be done away in the resurrection.

Objection: The condition of man and beast is the same, "For the condition of the children of men, and the condition of beasts are even as one condition unto them: As the one dieth, so dieth the other: for they have all one breath, and there is no excellency of man above the best; for all is vanity," (Ecclesiastes 3:19).

Solution: First, they are alike in dying, but not in the state after death. Secondly, it may be said, those words are the objection of the epicure, not the opinion of Solomon.

Secondly, it may add to our comfort, that the Lord is at hand, (Philippians 4:5) and that it is but a little season there to, (Revelation 6:11).

Thirdly, the present condition of our bodies even in the grave should comfort us: for

1. The covenant of God is of force even with them, as they lie in the dust of the earth, (Matthew 22:31-32).

2. The union with Christ hold still, (Colossians 1:18).

3. They are not dead, but sleep in Jesus, (1 Thessalonians 4:13).

Fourthly, woe to wicked men, even because of the resurrection: they shall sleep for a while in their bodies, but when they wake, they must be had away to execution. Those that have done evil shall rise unto shame, and contempt, and condemnation: their bodies shall rise in dishonor, deformity, passable, tormented with eternal and unutterable tortures, living in darkness without light, (living, I say forever, only to feel the pains of eternal dying) shut up in prison, and denied the comfort of the meanest creatures; it were well for them, if they never rose, (Revelation 20:14-15, Daniel 12:2, John 5:29).

CHAPTER 27:
Of the Last Judgment

"For we must all appear before the judgment seat of Christ, that every man may receive the things which are done in his body, according to that he hath done, whether it be good or evil," (2 Corinthians 5:10).

So we have considered the resurrection; the last judgment follows. The principles concerning the last judgment are these:

1. First, that there shall be a general judgment, "And Enoch also, the seventh from Adam, prophesied of such, saying: Behold the Lord cometh with thousands of saints: To give judgment against all men, and to rebuke all the ungodly among them of all their wicked deeds, which they have in an ungodly manner committed, and of all their cruel speakings, which wicked sinners have spoken against him," (Jude 1:14-15). "For he shall judge the world in righteousness, and shall judge the people with equity," (Psalm 9:8). "The God of Gods, even the Lord hath spoken, and called the earth from the rising up of the sun, unto the going down thereof," (Psalm 50:1). "And as it is appointed unto men, that they shall once die, and after that cometh the judgment," (Hebrews 9:27). "I beheld till the thrones were set up, and the Ancient of days did sit, whose garment was white as snow, and the hair of his head like the pure wool: his throne was like the fiery flame, and his wheels as burning fire: A fiery stream issued, and came forth from before him: thousand thousands ministered unto him, and ten thousand thousands stood before him: the judgment was set, and the books opened," (Daniel 7:9-10).

2. Secondly, that Christ shall be the Judge, and that in his human nature, "And he commanded us to preach unto the people, and to testify that it is he that is ordained of God a Judge of quick and dead," (Acts 10:42). "Because he hath appointed a day, in the which he will judge the world in righteousness by that man, whom he hath appointed, of which he hath given an assurance to all men, in that he raised him from the dead," (Acts 17:13). "I charge thee therefore before God, and before the Lord Jesus Christ, which shall judge the quick and dead at his appearing, and in his kingdom," (2 Timothy 4:1). "For the Father judgeth no man, but hath committed all judgment unto the Son," (John 5:22).

Objection. The Apostles shall judge the twelve tribes, (Matthew 19:28).

Solution. 1. The Apostles judge the twelve tribes by their faith and doctrine, the example of which shall take away all excuse from the Israelites. 2. They shall be as justices of peace on the bench, and consent to Christ's judgment.

Objection. The saints shall judge the world, (1 Corinthians 6:2).

Solution. As assessors with Christ, bearing witness to it, approving it, and assenting to it, as the Apostles before. 2. As they are members of Christ the Judge. 3. As their example shall be alleged to condemn the wicked.

Objection. But the Father and Holy Spirit judge too.

Solution. The Father does judge by the Son, as by his representative wisdom, "For the Father judgeth no man, but hath committed all judgment unto the Son," (John 5:22). "I saw in the night visions, and, behold, one like the Son of man came with the clouds of heaven, and came to the Ancient of days, and they brought him near before him. And there was given him dominion, and glory, and a kingdom, that all people, nations, and languages, should serve him: his dominion is an everlasting dominion, which shall not pass away, and his kingdom that which shall not be destroyed," (Daniel 7:13-14). Or in this way, that the authority of judging is common to the three persons, but the execution only proper to the Son.

3. Thirdly, all men shall be judged at that day: just and unjust; quick and dead; small and great, "To give judgment against all men, and to rebuke all the ungodly among them," (Jude 15). "For Christ therefore died and rose again, and revived, that he might be Lord both of the dead, and the quick," (Romans 14:9). "For we must all appear before the judgment seat of Jesus Christ," (2 Corinthians 5:10). "We shall all appear before the judgment seat of Jesus Christ," (Romans 14:10). "For he shall judge the world," (Psalm 9:8).

Objection. All men are believers or unbelievers; now the believers shall not come unto judgment: as appears, "Verily, verily I say unto you, he that heareth my word, and believeth in him that sent me, hath everlasting life, and shall not come into condemnation, but hath passed from death unto life," (John 5:24). And the unbeliever is condemned already, "He that believeth not is condemned already," (John 3:18).

Solution. The believer shall not come into the judgment of condemnation, and the unbeliever is condemned already in effect and substance: 1. In the counsel of God: 2. In the word of God: 3. In his own conscience, but yet the manifestation and finishing of this judgment remains to the last day.

4. Fourthly, all the secret things of men's natures or works shall be brought to light, "For nothing is secret, that shall not be evident: neither anything hid, that shall not be known, and come to light," (Luke 8:17). "Therefore judgment before the time, until the Lord come, who will lighten things that are hid in darkness, and make the counsel of the heart

manifest," (1 Corinthians 4:5). "And that day God shall judge the secrets of men by Jesus Christ," (Romans 2:16). And therefore it is called a day of revelation or declaration, (Romans 2:5).

5. Fifthly, it shall be at the last day, but the precise day and hour is not known to any men or angels; the proof for the like principle concerning the resurrection, serves for this place, (Matthew 24:36).

6. Sixthly, the judgment shall be most just and righteous, and all shall confess it, ("But why dost thou judge thy brother? or why dost thou despise thy brother? for we shall all appear before the judgment seat of Christ," (Romans 14:10). "For henceforth is laid up for me the crown of righteousness, which the Lord the righteous judge shall give me at that last day: and not to me only, but unto all them also which love his appearing," (2 Timothy 4:8). "But thou, after thine hardness, and heart that cannot repent, heapest unto thyself wrath against the day of wrath, and of the declaration of the just judgment of God," (Romans 2:5). "For he shall judge the world with righteousness, and shall judge the people with equity," (Psalm 9:8).

7. Seventhly, the judgment shall be according to men's works, "Every man shall receive the things which are done in his body, according to that he hath done, whether it be good or evil," (2 Corinthians 5:10). "Who will reward every man according to his works," (Romans 2:6).

Objection: We are justified by faith alone without works.

Solution: 1. Works are inquired after in the last judgment, as the signs of faith, and unbelief.

Solution 2: We are justified by faith only, but shall be judged by faith and works both together. In considering this, judgment does not serve to make men just who are unjust, but only to manifest to them that they are so indeed, which were this way in this life being truly justified.

The consideration of this should serve for diverse uses, and first for instruction, and so it should teach us,

1. First in general, speedily to repent of our sins, and it should stir us to all possible care of holy life, and to the love of all well doing, by which our reckoning might then be furthered, (Acts 17:31). "Seeing therefore that all these things must be dissolved, what manner of persons ought ye to be in holy conversation and godliness?" (2 Peter 3:11)."Wherefore beloved, seeing you look for such things, be diligent, that ye may be found of him in peace, without spot and blameless," (2 Peter 3:14). "That ye may discern things that differ from one another, that ye may be pure and without offense, until the day of Christ," (Philippians 1:10). "And teacheth us that we should deny ungodliness and worldly lusts and that we should live soberly, and righteously, and godly in this present world. Looking for the blessed hope and appearing of the glory of the mighty God, and of our Savior Jesus Christ," (Titus 2:12-13).

2. Secondly, in particular it should teach us,

1. Not to love earthly things, seeing they must all be consumed in that day in the fire.

2. To be patient under all wrongs, seeing we are assured there shall be vengeance rendered at that day, (2 Thessalonians 1:5-7, James 5:6-7, Philippians 4:5).

3. Thirdly, to take heed of rashness in judging other men: and men offend in censuring others;

1. When they inflict censures, and meddle over busily, or curiously with them that be without, "For what have I to do, to judge them which are without? (1 Corinthians 5:12).

2. When men speak evil of that which is good, and call good evil, "Woe unto them that speak good of evil, and evil of good; which put darkness for light, and light for darkness; that put bitter for sweet, and sweet for bitter," (Isaiah 5:20).

3. When men judge of things doubtful, as the hidden things of the heart, and the secret things of darkness, "Therefore judge nothing before the time, until the Lord come, who will lighten things that are hid in darkness, and make the counsels of the heart manifest," (1 Corinthians 4:5). And censure things in the worst sense.

4. When men uncharitably censure others about things indifferent, "Let not him that eateth, despise him that eateth not; and let not him which eateth not, judge him that eateth, for God hath received him. Who art thou that condemnest another man's servant? He standeth or falleth to his own master: yea he shall be established; for God is able to make him stand," (Romans 13:3-4). "Let us not therefore judge one another anymore, but use your judgment rather in this, that no man put an occasion to fall, or a stumbling block before his brother," (14:13).

5. When men commit, what they condemn, "Therefore thou art inexcusable, O man, whosoever thou art that judgest another, thou condemnest thyself, for thou that judgest, dost the same things. But we know that the judgment of God is according to truth, against them which commit such things," (Romans 2:1-2). Or being guilty of greater faults, condemn others for lesser, "Judge not, that ye be not judged. And why seest thou the mote that is in thy brother's eye, and perceivest not the beam that is in thine own eye," (Matthew 7:1-3).

6. When men make a fault worse than it is.

Fourthly, it should strike a fear into our hearts concerning God, and his dreadful majesty and justice; and make us afraid to offend him, and seek by all means to glorify him, whatever becomes of us and the world, "Saying with a loud voice; fear God, and give glory to him; for the hour of his judgment is come; and worship him that made heaven and earth, and the sea, and the fountain of waters," (Revelation 14:7).

Fifthly, we should be sober, in not inquiring into things not revealed, and look to the main business: as for the precise time, or place of the judgment, or from where the fire shall come that shall burn all, or what kind of throne it shall be, or what the sign of the Son of Man shall be, or such like; we believe that they shall be, but ought not to inquire when, where, or how they shall be.

Sixthly, chiefly this doctrine of the last judgment should compel in all of us a care so to live, that we may be sure to have comfort in that day: and that we shall be sure to find it;

1. If we believe in Jesus Christ, "Verily, verily, I say unto you, he that heareth my word, and believeth in him sent me, hath everlasting life, and shall not come into condemnation, but hath passed from death unto life," (John 5:24).

2. If we are sure to judge ourselves here, God will not condemn us with the world, "For if we would judge ourselves, we should not be judged," (1 Corinthians 11:31).

3. If we continually consult with the word of God, to see that our deeds are worked in God, "He that doth truth, cometh to the light, that his deeds might be made manifest, that they are wrought according to God," (John 3:19-21).

4. If we watch and pray always, that they pray much on earth, shall stand before Christ with comfort at that day, "Watch therefore and pray continually, that ye may be counted worthy to escape all these things that shall come to pass, and that ye may stand before the Son of Man," (Luke 21:36).

5. If we are merciful and loving, and bountiful to the godly in their distresses, (Matthew 25:31).

6. If we are sheep; sheep I say: 1. For being easily managed, so as we know, hear and are ruled by the voice of Christ, 2. For being sociable: a sheep will not be alone, nor sort with swine, 3. For profitableness that we are not idle, nor unfruitful, (Matthew 25, John 10).

7. If we can get the seal of the Spirit, as our earnest of final redemption at that day; the witness of the Spirit in this life will make all sure against that day, "The Spirit of promise is the earnest of our inheritance, until the redemption of the possession purchased unto the praise of his glory," (Ephesians 1:14). "For ye have not received the spirit of bondage to fear again, but ye have received the Spirit of adoption, whereby we cry Abba, Father," (Romans 8:15).

8. If we hold fast what we have, and do not lose what we have wrought, "Behold I come shortly, hold that which thou hast, that no man take thy crown," (Revelation 3:11). "Look to yourselves, that we lose not the things which we have done, but that we may receive a full reward," (2 John 8).

9. If we often receive the sacrament of the Lord's Supper with due preparation: for in this,

1. Christ familiarly converses with us, and is given to our nourishment to eternal life.

2. The outward elements are genuine pledges of the remission of all our sins.

3. We in it remember the death of Christ for us, and how he was judged for our sakes, and by it have our hearts settled against the fear of any severity from him.

4. In the right preparation of the sacrament, we prepare for the last judgment too; one work serves to both purposes.

5. The sacraments are God's broad seals, to assure us that we shall speed well at that day. So we have considered these uses for our instruction.

2. Secondly, this doctrine of the last judgment has singular terror in it to all impenitent sinners, which may be considered either more generally, or more particularly.

1. First, in general, it is terrible for them to hear and know that God has set them a day, and has given them final warning to repent; or else undoubtedly he will judge them with all severity, "Because he hath appointed a day, in the which we will judge the world in righteousness, by that man whom he hath appointed of which he hath given an assurance unto all men, in that he hath raised him from the dead," (Acts 17:31). "To give judgment against all men, and to rebuke all the ungodly among them of all their wicked deeds, which they have ungodly committed, and of all their cruel speaking which wicked sinners have spoken against him," (Jude 15). "But thou after thine hardness, and heart that cannot repent, heapest unto thyself wrath against the day of wrath, and of the declaration of the just judgment of God. Who will reward every man according to his works," (Romans 2:5).

2. Secondly, in particular, this terror is more grievous, if they consider either the distinct miseries shall then fall upon them or the several sins God has reserved to trial and punishment at that day. What heart can stand before the serious thoughts of these particulars?

1. They shall hear the thunders of Christ's fearful voice summoning them.

2. They shall be chased in by the angels before Christ, from all the four winds of heaven.

3. They shall be set at Christ's left hand, as a sign of miserable disgrace, (Matthew 25:33).

4. A fire shall devour before Christ, and it shall be tempestuous around him, "Our God shall come, and shall not keep silence; a fire shall devour before him, and a mighty tempest shall be moved round about him," (Psalm 50:3). "In flaming fire rendering vengeance unto them, that do not know God, and which obey not unto the Gospel of our Lord Jesus Christ," (2 Thessalonians 1:8).

5. They shall be everlastingly shamed, and before all the world, "And many of them, that sleep in the dust of the earth shall awake, some to everlasting life, and some to shame and perpetual contempt," (Daniel 12:2); when all their sins shall be discovered, and set in order before them, "These things hast thou done, and I held my tongue; therefore thou thoughtest, that I was like thee: but I will reprove thee, and set them in order before thee," (Psalm 50:21).

6. They shall be sentenced to eternal condemnation, containing in it,

1. Separation from God, Christ, and all the godly, "Go ye cursed," (Matthew 25:41).

2. Pain and anguish which is unutterable, "Tribulation and anguish shall be upon the soul of every man that doth evil: of the Jew first, and also of the Grecian," (Romans 2:9).

3. Fellowship with the devil and his angels, (Matthew 25:41).

Objection. Someone might say, it is appointed, as certain, as that men shall die, "And as it is appointed unto men, that they shall once die, and after that cometh the judgment," (Hebrews 9:27). "Because he hath appointed a day, in the which he will judge the world in righteousness," (Acts 17:31).

Besides, the terrible plagues, which have been and are in the world, shows that God is extremely angry with sin, and will call to judgment; such as the drowning of the old world, burning of Sodom, swallowing up of Korah, Dathan, and such; the neglect of the Gentiles, the rejection of the Jews, the punishing of Christ, the afflictions of the godly, the wars, pestilences, famines, and those that are in the world.

And they themselves may guess somewhat at it, by the sharpness of the word, the accusing of the conscience, the checks of the Spirit, and the fearful terrors of conscience which fall upon some men.

Objection. But God, we hope, will be merciful.

Solution. It is a day of wrath, not of mercy; the date of mercy will be then out, "But thou after thine hardness and heart, which cannot repent, heapest unto thyself wrath against the day of wrath, and of the declaration of the just judgment of God," (Romans 2:5).

Objection. But God says nothing to me all this while: I escape, and am not troubled; I discern no way that God is displeased with me.

Solution 1: Seas of wrath hand over your head daily, though you do not discern them, "He that believeth in the Son hath everlasting life, and he that obeyeth not the Son, shall not see the life, but the wrath of God abideth on him," (John 3:36).

Solution 2: Many signs of God's displeasure are upon your soul, though you do not feel them. It is one extreme curse to be left off to such a spirit of slumber.

Solution 3: Though God does not yet show to you his displeasure, yet he will awake to your judgment, "These things hast thou done, and I held my tongue; therefore thou thought that I was like thee: but I will reprove thee, and set them in order before thee," (Psalm 50:31).

Objection. But I may find some means to help myself at that day.

Solution: Riches will not avail in the day of wrath, "For God's wrath is, lest he should take thee away in thine abundance: for no multitude of gifts can deliver thee. Will he regard thy riches? He regardeth not gold, nor all them that excel in strength," (Job 36:18-19). And there shall be none to deliver, "O consider this, ye that forget God; lest I tear you in pieces, and there be none that can deliver you," (Psalm 50:22).

Objection: But then I may repent.

Solution: No, as death leaves you, so shall judgment find you; it is a day of the declaration of the righteous judgment of God, "But thou after thine hardness, and heart, that cannot repent, heapest unto thyself wrath, and of the declaration of the just judgment of God," (Romans 2:5). "For we must all appear before the judgment seat of Christ, that every man receive the things which are done in his body, according to that he hath done whether it be good or evil," (2 Corinthians 5:10).

Objection: But there is a world of people in the same case.

Solution: He will judge all the ungodly, he does not care for the multitude, "To give judgment against all men, and to rebuke all the ungodly amongst them of all their wicked deeds, which they have ungodly committed, and of all their cruel speaking, which wicked sinners have spoken against him," (Jude 15).

Besides, he has plagued multitudes, as the old world, and he can easily do execution; for he comes with thousand thousands of his angels, "And Enoch also, the seventh from Adam, prophesied of such, saying, Behold, the Lord cometh with thousands of his saints," (Jude 14).

Objection: But who knows my faults?

Solution: The hidden things of darkness, and the secrets of men's hearts shall then be discovered, "Therefore judge nothing before the time until the Lord come, who will lighten things, that are hid in darkness, and make the counsels of the hearts manifest, and then shall every man have praise of God," (1 Corinthians 4:5).

Objection: By what evidence can I be convinced? God may forget my faults before then.

Solution: No, God has them written in his book of remembrance with a pen of iron, and a point of a diamond, "The sin of Judah is written with a pen of iron, and with the point of a diamond, and graven upon the table of your hearts, and upon the horns of your altars," (Jeremiah 17:1). And evidence will be easy to be had upon the opening of these books, "And I saw the dead both great and small stand before God, and the books were opened: and another book was opened, which is the book of life, and the dead were judged of those things which are written in the books, according to their works," (Revelation 20:12).

Besides, the heavens will declare his righteousness, (Psalm 50:6). And the creatures abused by them will give an evidence against them, (Jeremiah 17:1). And the word that men have heard shall judge them. And their own consciences shall be dilated, and be instead of a thousand witnesses: and the Spirit of God that has so often reproved the world of sin, can easily accuse them, "And when he is come, he will reprove the world of sin, and of righteousness, and of judgment," (John 16:8).

Objection: I know of no great fault by myself.

Solution: Though you forget your sins; yet Christ will remember them, (Matthew 25). It will not serve the turn to say, when did we so?

Objection: But I never did Christ any wrong.

Solution: You have many ways sinned against Christ, though your careless heart does not perceive it: but if you had not, yet inasmuch as you have done wrong to Christians, you have done it to Christ, (Matthew 25).

Objection: But I have done much good in the world.

Solution: If you have not had true faith and love and repentance, it shall not avail you, as these places show, "And though I feed the poor with all my goods, and though I give my body, that I be burned, and have not love, it profiteth me nothing," (1 Corinthians 13:3).

Objection: But we never had such means of knowledge, as others have had.

Solution: Those that have sinned without the law, shall be judged without the law; and those that have sinned under the law, shall be judged by the law, "For as many as have sinned without the law, shall perish also without the law; and as many as have sinned in the law, shall be judged by the law," (Romans 2:12).

Objection: But it is a great while later.

Solution: It is not, for the Lord is at hand, "Now the end of all things is at hand; be you therefore sober, and watching in prayer," (1 Peter 4:7). "Be ye also patient therefore, and settle your hearts; for the coming of the Lord draweth near," (James 5:8).

Besides, the signs of the last judgment are the most of them accomplished already; Antichrist is revealed, and almost pulled down, (2 Thessalonians 2, 1 John 2:18). The world has been full of spirits of deceivers, (1 Timothy 4:1). The sins of the last age are everywhere at the full. Iniquity abounds, (2 Timothy 3:1, Matthew 24:12). The powers of heaven are shaken, which appears by the often eclipses of sun and moon; and by the uncertainty of the seasons both in summer and winter,

(Matthew 24:29). The sea roars and is outrageous; men are secure now as in the days of Noah, (Matthew 24:37).

3. You wish that it was further off: yet the day of death, which is the day of your particular judgment, is not far off.

Objection. But yet sure there will be some kind of warning.

Solution. No, he will come suddenly, as the thief in the night, "For ye yourselves know perfectly that the day of the Lord shall come, even as a thief in the night. For when they shall say, peace and safety, then shall come upon them sudden destruction, as the travail upon a woman with child, and they shall not escape," (1 Thessalonians 5:2-3). "And knew nothing, till the flood came, and took them all away; so shall also the coming of the Son of Man be," (Matthew 24:39).

And rather should men be affected with the terror of this day, and by it be persuaded to repentance:

1. Because God will be Judge himself, (Psalm 50:6) and therefore there can be no appeal, he being the supreme Judge.

2. Because it is a final sentence, there will be no time of respite, or change, or revocation.

3. Because they shall be judged by him, whom they have so much despised, and wronged, "Behold, he cometh in the clouds, and every eye shall see him; yea, even they which pierced him through, and all kindreds of the earth shall wail before him," (Revelation 1:7-8).

4. Because God's proceedings shall all be cleared, and every tongue shall confess, that God has nothing but justice, "It is a day of the declaration of the just judgment of God," (Romans 2:5, 14:11): And this justice will the more appear,

1. By the equity of God's dealing: they have had their day of sin, and therefore we should consider that he should have his day of wrath, (Romans 2:5).

2. By the consideration of his patience, what a wonderful while has God deferred this last judgment, "The Lord is not slack concerning his promise, as some men count slackness, but is patient toward us, and would have no man to perish, but would all men to come to repentance," (2 Peter 3:9). "Or despisest thou the riches of his bountifulness, and patience, and longsuffering, not knowing that the bountifulness of God leadeth thee to repentance," (Romans 2:4).

3. God will then show a world of offenses in every wicked man that are now not known.

4. God will then unfold the secrets of his counsel, and bring forth exquisite reasons of his proceedings, which are now like a great deep to us, "O the deepness of the riches, both of the wisdom, and knowledge of God! How unsearchable are his judgments, and his ways past finding out!" (Romans 11:33).

And as this doctrine is terrible, in respect of the parts of their misery, and in respect of the taking off of all objections: so is it, because the particular sinners are particularly mentioned in Scripture, that shall be sure to speed ill at that day: for Christ with terror will then judge,

1. The man of sin, who shall be sure to be consumed with the breath of his mouth, though he lord it over all that is called God, for a time, (2 Thessalonians 2:4).

2. All that worship the beast, and receive his mark, shall be cast into the lake that burns with fire and brimstone, (Revelation 19:20, 14:9-10).

3. All atheistic mockers of religion, and the coming of Christ, (2 Peter 3:3).

4. All false teachers, which bring in damnable heresies, (2 Peter 2:1).

5. All apostates that sin willingly after they have received the truth, "For if we sin willingly after we have

received the knowledge of the truth, there remaineth no more sacrifice for sins. But a fearful looking for of judgment, and violent fire, which shall devour the adversaries," (Hebrews 10:26-27).

6. All goats, that is, unruly people that will not be kept within the bounds of Christ's government, (Matthew 25:32).

7. All hypocrites shall then be unmasked, "Take heed to yourselves of the leaven of the Pharisees, which is hypocrisy. For there is nothing covered, that shall not be revealed, neither hid, that shall not be known," (Luke 12:1-2, Psalm 50:17).

8. All railers shall receive the punishment of their ungodly words, "To give judgment against all men, and to rebuke all the ungodly among them of all their wicked deeds, which they have ungodly committed, and of all their cruel speaking, which wicked sinners have spoken against him.

9. All censorious and master-like men, that judge other men in what they are guilty themselves, "Therefore thou art inexcusable, O man, whosoever thou art, that judgest: for in that thou judgest another, thou condemnest thyself, for thou that judgest dost the same things," (Romans 2:1). "And thinkest thou this, O thou man, that judgest them which do such things, and doest the same, that thou shalt escape the judgment of God?" (Romans 2:3). "My brethren, be not many masters, knowing that we shall receive the greater condemnation," (James 3:1).

10. All merciless and covetous rich men, "Go to now ye rich men, weep, and howl for your miseries, that shall come upon you. Your riches are corrupt, and your garments are moth-eaten. Your gold and silver is cankered, and the rust of them shall be a witness against you, and shall eat your flesh as it were fire, ye have heaped up treasures for the last days. Ye have lived in pleasure on the earth, and in wantonness; ye have nourished

your hearts as in a day of slaughter," (James 5:1-3,5). "Then shall he say unto them on the left hand, depart from me, ye cursed into everlasting fire, which is prepared for the devil and his angels. For I was hungered, and you gave me no meat; I thirsted, and ye gave me no drink," (Matthew 25:41-42). "For there shall be judgment merciless, to him that sheweth no mercy," (James 2:13).

11. All whoremongers and adulterers, "Marriage is honorable among all and the bed undefiled: but whoremongers and adulterers God will judge," (Hebrews 13:4).

12. All drunkards and epicures, "Take heed to yourselves, lest at any time your hearts be oppressed with surfeiting and drunkenness, and cares of this life, and lest that day come upon you unawares," (Luke 21:34).

13. All deceitful people with their scant measures, and false weights, "Are yet the treasures of wickedness in the house of the wicked, and the scant measure that is abominable? Shall I justify the wicked balances, and the bag of deceitful weights?" (Mark 6:10-11).

14. All liars, and all that love lies, "But the fearful, and unbelieving, and the abominable, and murderers, and whoremongers, and sorcerers, and idolaters, and all liars, shall have their part in the lake which burneth with fire and brimstone, which is the second death," (Revelation 21:8). "For without shall be dogs, and enchanters, and whoremongers, and murderers, and idolaters, and whosoever loveth, or maketh lies," (Revelation 22:15).

15. Lastly, all that disobey the Gospel, "In flaming fire, rendering vengeance unto them that do not know God, and which obey not unto the Gospel of our Lord Jesus Christ," (2 Thessalonians 1:8). And so much for considering terror.

Lastly, the doctrine of the last judgment should be exceedingly comfortable to all the godly, and that in many respects:

1. First, if they shall consider who shall be their Judge, even he that is their brother, husband, advocate, head, and redeemer; he that was judged for their sakes; and therefore they need to fear no hard sentence from him.

2. Secondly, if they consider the present assurance of hope.

1. For first, has Christ not given them many promises, that it shall go well with them at that day?

2. Has Christ not justified them already, and absolved them from all their sins? (Romans 3:24-25).

3. Have they not received the earnest of the Spirit, and the seal of the sacraments? (2 Corinthians 1:21-22, 2 Corinthians 5:5).

4. Have they not judged themselves, and therefore are they not free from condemnation with the world? (1 Corinthians 11:31-32).

5. They have been judged already, the afflictions of this life will be accounted sufficient unto them, (1 Peter 4:17).

They may trust their souls to God: and that God, that has begun his good work in them, will perform it till the day of Christ, (Philippians 1:5-6, 1 Corinthians 1:8).

3. Thirdly, if they consider the benefits they shall attain unto at that day: for Christ will be made marvelous in all those that believe, (2 Thessalonians 1:10). They shall have honor, and praise; their innocence shall be cleared, and miseries and sins ended. And when Christ shall appear, then shall we also appear with him in glory, (Colossians 3:4).

4. Fourthly, if they consider the circumstances of the judgment, as,

1. The nearness of the time should make them hold up their heads, (Matthew 24:22,33). "Let your patient mind be known unto all men, the Lord is at hand," (Philippians 4:5). "Be ye also patient therefore, and settle your hearts for the coming of the Lord draweth near, (James 5:8).

2. The greatness of the assembly, before whom they shall be so much graced by Christ, they shall be honored before all men and angels.

3. The condition of the sentence, it shall be a final sentence never to be revoked, but acknowledged to all eternity.

4. And besides, they shall have this favor, that nothing shall be remembered except for goodness in good men: their sins shall not be mentioned to them, (Matthew 25:34, 41-42).

CHAPTER 28:
Of the Glory of Heaven

"But as it is written, the things which eye hath not seen, neither ear heard, neither came into man's heart, are, which God hath prepared for them that love him," (1 Corinthians 2:9).

We have considered the principles that concern the resurrection, and the last judgment: The principles that concern the glory of heaven follow.

There are four principles concerning the glory of heaven.

1. The first concerns its greatness. It is unspeakable, and in respect of us here on earth, incomprehensible, (1 Corinthians 2:9). "Dearly beloved, now are we sons of God, but yet it doth not appear what we shall be, and we know that when we shall appear, we shall be like him; for we shall see him as he is," (1 John 3:2). "For ye are dead, and your life is hidden with Christ in God. When Christ which is our life shall appear, then shall we also appear with him in glory," (Colossians 3:3-4). "How that he was taken up into paradise, and heard words which cannot be spoken, which are not possible for man to utter," (2 Corinthians 12:4). "Let him that hath an ear to hear, what the Spirit saith unto the churches: to him that overcometh will I give to eat of the manna that is hid, and will give him a white stone, and in the stone a new name written, which no man knoweth saving he that receiveth it," (Revelation 2:17). "Thou wilt shew me the path of life, in thy presence is the fullness of joy, and at thy right hand there are pleasures forevermore," (Psalm 16:11). "How great is thy goodness, which thou hast laid

up for them that fear thee, and done to them that trust in thee, even before the sons of men?" (Psalm 31:19).

2. The second concerns its continuance, and so it is eternal; and therefore this life is called *eternal* life, and immortality, "And these shall go into everlasting pain, and the righteous into life eternal," (Matthew 25:46). "But is now made manifest by the appearing of our Savior Jesus Christ, who has abolished death, and hath brought life and immortality unto light, through the Gospel," (2 Timothy 1:10). "To an inheritance immortal, and undefiled, and that fadeth not away, reserved in heaven for you," (2 Corinthians 5:1).

3. The third concerns its cause. Heaven is the gift of God, and proceeds only from his free grace, and not for any merit in us, "Fear not little flock, for it is your Father's good pleasure to give you a kingdom," (Luke 12:32). "But when the bountifulness and love of God our Savior toward man appeared; not for our righteousness, but according to his mercy he saved us," (Titus 3:4). "For God so loved the world, that he hath given his only begotten Son, that whosoever believeth in him should not perish, but have everlasting life," (John 3:16). "For the wages of sin is death; but the gift of God is eternal life, through Jesus Christ our Lord," (Romans 6:23). (1 Peter 1, the entire chapter).

4. The fourth concerns the persons that shall enjoy it: only the elect of God obtain this glory, "This say I brethren, that flesh and blood cannot inherit the kingdom of God, neither doth corruption inherit incorruption," (1 Corinthians 15:50). "And there shall enter into it none unclean thing, neither whatsoever worketh abomination, or lies, but they which are written in the Lambs book of life," (Revelation 21:27). "Know ye not that the unrighteous shall not inherit the kingdom of God? be not deceived: Neither fornicators, nor wantons, nor

buggers," (1 Corinthians 6:9). "That is to them which by continuance in well doing, seek glory, and honor, and immortality, eternal life," (Romans 2:7). "But to every man that doth good shall be glory, and honor, and peace, to the Jew first, and also to the Grecian," (Romans 2:10).

The uses follow, and are either for instruction, or for consolation.

First, for instruction: and then the doctrine of the glory of heaven should work diverse impressions on their hearts.

1. We should with all earnestness importune God to enable us to behold by the effectualness of contemplation, the greatness of that joy, which is provided for us in heaven: we are naturally extremely unable for its contemplation, we should implore God by his Spirit to force open our eyes, and make us able to stand and gaze with admiration at the glory to come, (Ephesians 1:18-19, Romans 5:2-3).

2. Our hearts should be fired with an ardency of desire, and endeavor to praise the glorious and free grace of God, which has without our deserts appointed us unto such glory; we can never walk worthy of heaven, until we are fitted to a daily and affectionate praise of God's love to us in it. All ages should stand and wonder at such rich grace and tender kindness of God in Jesus Christ, (Ephesians 1:6, 2:7).

3. Thirdly, it should raise up in us a wonderful estimation of the godly, who are therefore the only excellent ones, because as princes of God they are born heirs to so great a kingdom. No meanness of their outward condition should abate of our reverence to them, that are so rich in faith, and heirs of such glory, (Psalm 6:3, James 2:5).

And seeing we must live with them forever, we should choose them, as the most happy companions of our lives here, and receive them as Christ received us to glory, (Romans 15:7, 1

John 4:7, 17). And live in all peace with them, (Ephesians 4:23). And for this reason husbands should make much of their godly wives, as heirs with them of the same grace of God, (1 Peter 3:8). And masters should use with all respect their religious servants, knowing that of the Lord, their very servants shall receive the reward of inheritance, (Colossians 3:23-24).

4. Fourthly, it should exceedingly raise the price of godliness, and make us with all hearty affection devote ourselves to well doing, seeing there is such an invaluable gain that arises unto such as with patience and painfulness continue in doing good: we should be abundant in the work of the Lord; if for no reason, yet because of the great reward in heaven, (1 Corinthians 15:58, Romans 2:7,10).

5. Fifthly, it should make us to take off our affections from the world, with disdain and indignation at ourselves for being so foolish, as to settle our hearts on things below. And since necessity enjoins us to use the world, this religious hope should make us use it, as if we used it not, expressing all sobriety and temperance, and contempt of those transitory things, and setting our hearts there, where those matchless treasures are. What profit is it to win all this world, if our souls are shut out of heaven? And what loss can it be, if we lose the world to come? This doctrine should make us feelingly know and profess ourselves to be strangers and pilgrims here; and desire to be no other, than such, as long to be absent from here, that we may be present with the Lord in this glorious place, (1 Corinthians 7:31, Colossians 3:1-2, 1 Peter 1:13, Matthew 6:19-20, Matthew 16:25-26, Hebrews 11:13, 2 Corinthians 5:6).

6. Sixthly, we should be especially careful to be all that, that is required to eternal life.

And so in general we must be sure that we are born again, else Christ is peremptory, we cannot enter into the kingdom of heaven, (John 3:5). Heaven is an inheritance, and therefore we must first be sons. That glory must penetrate into our hearts by its beams, so as we are changed from glory to glory, (2 Corinthians 3:18). We must enter into the first degree of eternal life, and that is in this life, we must bear the image of Christ.

And in particular, we must distinctly look to these things:

1. We must be careful to be provided of the means to teach us the way to heaven; we must labor for the food that endures to eternal life, (John 6:37). As knowing that the preaching of the Gospel is the power of God to salvation, (Romans 1:16, 10:14).

2. We must seriously study the mysteries of this kingdom, and keep ourselves close to profitable things, which may edify us, (Matthew 13:11, Titus 3:8-9).

3. We must purge ourselves as he is pure, we must seriously, and soundly employ ourselves in the duties of mortification of our corruptions, "And every man that has this hope in him, purgeth himself, as he is pure," (1 John 3:3).

4. We must be sure that the tempter does not deceive us in our faith; for that is our evidence for those things, which are not seen, and that makes them (as it were) present, "Now faith is the ground of things which are hoped for, and the evidence of things which are not seen," (Hebrews 11:1). "Even for this cause when I could no longer forbear, I sent him that I might know of your faith; lest the tempter had tempted you in any sort, and that our labor had been in vain," (1 Thessalonians 3:5). "That the trial of your faith, being much more precious than gold that perishes, though it be tried with fire, might be found unto praise, and honor, and glory, at the appearing of Jesus Christ," (1 Peter 1:7). "Prove yourselves, whether you are

in the faith: examine yourselves, know ye not your own selves, how that Jesus Christ is in you, except you be reprobates?" (2 Corinthians 13:5).

For by faith Christ lives in us, (Galatians 2:20).

5. We must be sure, we are not ashamed of Christ in this world, and that we do not deny him here on earth, but contrary to this, "Whosoever therefore shall confess also before my Father, which is in heaven. But whosoever shall deny me before men, him will I also deny before my Father, which is in heaven," (Matthew 10:32-33).

6. We must get the earnest of this inheritance, which is the spirit of promise: for that will establish us, (Ephesians 1:14, 2 Corinthians 1:22-23).

For when God gives glory in heaven, then the Spirit of glory "rests upon men in this life," (1 Peter 4:14).

And the Spirit is our earnest, either by anointing us with saving grace, (for they assure us as infallibly of this kingdom, as the oil poured on the kings, assured them of their kingdom) or by refreshing, and satisfying our hearts, in hearing the promises, or receiving the sacraments, or answering our prayers: But in all this we must remember these things:

1. To do this work first: first, seek the kingdom of God, (Matthew 6:33) do not defer the time to the last gasp.

2. To do it constantly. Let him that is righteous be righteous still, (Revelation 22).

3. Praying in the Holy Spirit, and keeping ourselves in the love of God, (Jude 20-21).

4. To do it violently. Heaven should suffer violence, (Matthew 11:12).

5. To do it humbly, renouncing all our merits, and ascribing all to the free grace of God, and the merits of Jesus Christ, (Romans 6:23, Ephesians 2:8-9).

For heaven is an inheritance, and therefore comes by favor, not by purchase; and besides, we are adopted children too, and not natural.

6. Having finished all things, to stand fast, and hope perfectly for the grace of God to be brought to us at the revelation of Jesus Christ, (1 Peter 1:13). Secondly, these principles may serve for singular consolation, and so,

1. Against the instability of this present life, while we look upon our abiding city in heaven. In this way the patriarchs comforted themselves, (Hebrews 11:13).

2. Against the grief for the death of our friends, why do we sorrow for them, that are so happy?

3. Against the many afflictions of this life, the fear and care of which should be swallowed with the hope of eternal life, as these places show, "For I count, that the afflictions of this present time, are not worthy of the glory which shall be shown to us," (Romans 8:18). "For our light affliction, which is but for a moment, causeth unto us a far most excellent, and eternal weight of glory, while we look not on the things which are seen, but on the things which are not seen, for the things which are seen are temporal; but the things which are not seen, are eternal," (2 Corinthians 4:17-18).

4. Against the fear of death: for these principles teach us to believe that the dead are blessed, "Then I heard a voice from heaven saying unto me; Write, Blessed are the dead, which hereafter die in the Lord: even so saith the Spirit: for they rest from their labors, and their works follow them," (Revelation 14:13). And that this death will be quickly swallowed up of victorious life, "The sting of death is sin, and the strength of sin is the law. But thanks be to God, which hath given us victory through our Lord Jesus Christ," (1 Corinthians 15:16-17).

These comforts will be more abundant, if we consider, either, first, the particulars of this glory; secondly, or its properties.

1. For the first, our glory in heaven may be so shadowed out; it consists of perfection of holiness and happiness.

Our holiness shall then be perfect, we shall be without spot or wrinkle, (Ephesians 5:27). God's people shall then be all righteous, "Thy people also shall be all righteous," (Isaiah 60:21). And this perfection shall be both of nature, and of action.

In nature we shall be perfectly holy, which may be considered in respect of the holiness.

First, of our souls; secondly, of our bodies; thirdly, of our soul and body together.

First, in our souls there shall be,

1. Exquisite knowledge; we shall then know as we are known, when that which is in part is done away; we shall no more understand as children, but shall have our minds enlightened above the knowledge of Prophets and Apostles in this world; for God himself shall be our everlasting light, " But when that which is perfect is come, then that which is in part shall be abolished. When I was a child, I spake as a child, I understood as a child: but when I became a man, I put away childishness, or childish things: For now we see through a glass darkly, but then shall we face to face; now I know in part, but then shall I know, even as I am known," (1 Corinthians 13:10-12). "Thou shalt have no more sun to shine by day, neither shall the brightness of the moon shine unto thee: for the Lord shall be thine everlasting light, and thy God thy glory," (Isaiah 60:19).

2. Freedom of will, when all the impediments of desire and endeavors shall be taken off, which now as fetters hinder

us in communion with God, and as cords, hail us after vanity; where it shall be also as easy to do good, as to desire it.

3. Unspeakable charity; our hearts being filled with all those affections that are now any way required in the Word of God, either toward God or man, "Love doth never fall away, though that prophesying be abolished, or the tongues cease, or knowledge vanish away," (1 Corinthians 13:8). What is now the life of our lives more, than to love and to be loved? This earthly love is but a spark in comparison.

Secondly, in our bodies, there shall be a perfect conformity of all the members for the service of God and the soul, they shall be no more weapons of unrighteousness, as they have been (Romans 6:13, 19).

Thirdly, in both body and soul, there shall be,

1. The perfect vision of the admirable beauties of God, which of itself is of more worth than the possession of the whole world, and this vision of God shall not only be mental by contemplation, of which (2 Corinthians 12:2) but also corporeal; for so Job avouches "For I am sure my redeemer liveth, and he shall stand the last on earth. And though after my skin, worms destroy this body: yet shall I see God in my flesh, Whom I myself shall see, and my eyes behold, and none other for me, though my reins are consumed within me," (Job 19:25-27). We shall then see him perfectly in the creatures, and have him perfectly in ourselves, and behold the Trinity in its glory after a way now unutterable.

2. The perfection of the image of God in both: we shall then be, as he is, partaking perfectly of the divine nature, (1 John 3:2, 2 Peter 1:4) which is signified by those pure white garments, mentioned in Revelation 3:4-5, 6:11, 7:13, and 19:8. In this way shall we be perfect in nature.

The perfection of our actions, or obedience shall then serve God, and love our brethren without all defect. We shall praise God with the angels to all eternity: for that shall be the main outward service of God: for prayer shall then cease, (Revelation 4:10-11). In this way, there shall be a perfection of holiness. The perfection of happiness shall have in it diverse things.

1. The first part of our felicity is acknowledgement in the kingdom of heaven; which is a work of Christ, declaring us in particular to be elected of God, and his children, and friends. And this is more comfortable, because we shall so be proclaimed the heirs apparent of heaven before God, and all his holy angels, "Whosoever therefore shall confess me before men, him will I confess also before my Father which is in heaven," (Matthew 10:32).

2. Glorious liberty reserved for the sons of God unto that day, of which (Romans 8:21).

And this liberty may be considered in two ways, from what we shall be free, and to what we shall be free.

1. First, from the torments and miseries of the damned in hell, we shall have an eternal discharge from that most fearful place, which is promised us already in this life, "Now then there is no condemnation to them that are in Christ Jesus, which walk not after the flesh, but after the Spirit," (Romans 8:1). "And death and hell were cast into the lake of fire: this is the second death," (Revelation 20:14).

2. Secondly, from the displeasure of God; he will never be angry with us anymore, there shall be no more curse, or *anathema*, "And there shall be no more curse, but the throne of God and of the Lamb shall be in it, and his servants shall serve him," (Revelation 22:3).

3. Thirdly, from sin, and the power to sin: our holiness shall be better than Adam's in paradise; he might sin, but we shall be confirmed, as the angels of heaven. So, as we shall not only be free from sin, but from the possibility to sin, (Ephesians 5:26).

4. Fourthly, from all adversary power; we shall never more be molested by devils, nor by wicked men, either spiritual or corporeal. There shall be a perpetual triumph without war; all our enemies shall be cast into the lake of fire, (Revelation 21:8, 20:14, 22:3). As we shall not lose a friend because there is no death; so we shall not fear an enemy.

5. Fifthly, from all infirmity in our natures; as from ignorance, and all disabilities, from sorrow, discouragement, hardness of heart, fear, and worries, "And God shall wipe away all tears from their eyes, and there shall be no more death, neither sorrow, neither crying, neither shall there be any more pain; for the first things are passed," (Revelation 21:4). And so also from all such graces, as suppose either imperfection in us: such as faith, hope, and repentance: or misery in the creatures without us, as grief, anger, fear, hatred, and the like, (1 Corinthians 13).

6. Sixthly, from all inferiority, and subjection, and servitude, none shall be under the jurisdiction of others: all economical, political, and ecclesiastical relations shall then cease. We shall sit down with Abraham, Isaac, and Jacob in the kingdom of heaven, (Matthew 8:11).

7. Seventhly, from all labor and affliction of life. Their labors shall cease, and afflictions shall be cast into the sea, they shall enjoy an eternal Sabbath, the true Canaan, "Then I heard a voice from heaven, saying unto me; Write, blessed art the dead, which hereafter die in the Lord, even so saith the Spirit, for they rest from their labors, and their works follow them.

"There remaineth therefore a rest to the people of God," (Hebrews 4:9). "And to you which are troubled, rest with us, when the Lord Jesus shall shew himself from heaven with his mighty angels," (2 Thessalonians 1:7). And by labors, I understand also the pains or difficulties we are at, even about the service of God: for God shall be all in all.

8. Eighthly, from all shame and blushing. There shall be nothing but honor and praise to all eternity: where in this world the inward shame of some offense imputed, or committed, make life itself many times a burden, and there is little ease to the mind, but in remembrance of the day of Christ, when it shall be removed.

9. Ninthly, from all envy; envy is said to be bitter, (1 Corinthians 3:3). But when charity shall be perfect, then shall that property of not envying be made perfect too, (1 Corinthians 13).

10. Tenthly, from all interruptions both in holiness and felicity; which in this life is grievous, and arises many times from good things, and good persons, as well as evil.

11. Eleventhly, from all the means of a natural life, and from the inconveniences too: there shall be no need of meat, drink, sleep, marriage, raiment, medicine, nor the light of the sun: For there shall be no hunger, thirst, heat, cold, darkness, or the like grievances, but we shall live as the angels of heaven.

And so, in a word we shall be free from the first things, (Revelation 2:4). So much for what we shall be free from. Now follows, what we shall be free to.

1. First, we shall be free of heaven, the most holy place, "Seeing therefore brethren, that by the blood of Jesus we may be bold to enter into the holy place," (Hebrews 10:19).

- Paradise: "Then Jesus said unto him, verily I say unto thee, this day thou shalt be with me in paradise," (Luke 23:43).

- Our Father's house: "In my Father's house are many dwelling places: if it were not so, I would not have told you, I go to prepare a place for you," (John 14:2).

- The new Jerusalem: "And I saw the holy city, the new Jerusalem, come down from God out of heaven, prepared as a bride trimmed for her husband," (Revelation 21:2).

- The heaven of heavens, which for lightness, largeness, pureness, delightfulness, and all praises of a place almost infinitely excels all this visible world. Nor shall the godly be restrained only to heaven, but they shall be free of the new earth, wherein dwells righteousness "But we look for a new heaven, and a new earth, according to his promise, wherein dwelleth righteousness," (2 Peter 3:13).

2. Secondly, we shall be free to the enjoying of the happy society of all the glorious saints and angels of heaven, "But ye are come unto the mount Zion and to the city of the living God; the celestial Jerusalem, and to the company of innumerable angels. And to the congregation in heaven, and to God the Judge of all, and to the Spirit of just and perfect men.

3. Thirdly, to the glorious presence of God, and the Lamb; we shall always dwell in the King's presence, "And I heard a great voice out of heaven, saying, behold the tabernacle of God is with men, and he will dwell with them, and they shall be his people, and God himself shall be their God with them," (Revelation 21:3). "And there shall be no more curse; but the throne of God, and of the Lamb shall be in it, and his servants shall serve him. And they shall see his face, and his name shall be in their foreheads," (Revelation 22:3-4).

4. Fourthly, to all the treasures of heaven; which are inexpressible, shadowed out by some comparisons; as by being free to eat of the tree of life, "In the midst of the street of it, and of either side of the river was the tree of life, which bare twelve

manner of fruits, and gave fruit every month, and leaves of the tree served to heal the nations with," (Revelation 22:2).

As also by being free to drink of the water of life freely, "And he said unto me, It is done, I am Alpha and Omega, the beginning and the end, and I will give to him that is athirst of the well of the waters of life freely," (Revelation 21:6); even out of a river, that is pure as crystal, "And he showed me a pure river of water of life, clear as crystal, proceeding out of the throne of God, and of the Lamb," (Revelation 22:1). We should consider this and other things like them. So, we have considered liberty.

3. The third part of our felicity in heaven is majesty; all the godly shall be there seated as princes in thrones of majesty, and prince-like splendor, being crowned with crowns of glory; which glory shall be so great, that the kings of the earth are supposed to bring all their glory and honor to it, and yet all too little to shadow out this exceeding glory of all the saints, "To him that overcometh will I grant to sit with me in my throne, even as I overcome, and sit with my father in his throne," (Revelation 3:21). "For henceforth is laid up for me the crown of righteousness, which the Lord shall give me at that day: and not to me only, but unto all them also that love his appearing," (2 Timothy 4:8). "And the people which are saved, shall walk in the light of it, and the kings of the earth shall bring their glory and honor unto it," (Revelation 21:24).

Which as it imports a perfection of splendor in every saint, so it does not dissolve the degrees or orders of glory, every man shall be advanced in his own lot, "But go thou thy way, till the end be; for thou shalt rest and stand up in thy lot at the end of the days," (Daniel 12:13). "There are also heavenly bodies, and earthly bodies; but the glory of the heavenly is one, and the glory of the earthly is another. Patriarchs, Prophets,

Evangelists, Martyrs," (1 Corinthians 15:40) shall not lack their eminency in heaven.

4. The fourth is dominion, and rule over all creatures; and which we lost in Adam, shall be perfectly restored in heaven, after the last judgment, "For he that overcometh unto the end, to him will I give power over nations," (Revelation 2:26).

5. The fifth is possession of all the pleasures which are at God's right hand, unutterable joys, rivers of pleasures. This is that which in a sparing language is called the time of refreshing, "Amend your lives therefore, and turn, that your sins may be put away, when the time of refreshing shall come from the presence of the Lord," (Acts 3:19). "Thou wilt shew me the path of life: in thy presence is the fulness of joy; and at thy right hand are pleasures forevermore," (Psalm 16:11). For if the joy of the godly in this life is called, "A joy unspeakable and glorious," (1 Peter 1:17) and if "the Lord give them drink out of the river of thy pleasures in this world," (Psalm 36:8-9). How much more shall it exceed all language in heaven, called the master's joy!

The felicities which I have here mentioned, are for the most part common both to soul and body.

Now there is a peculiar felicity in heaven belonging to the bodies of men, which consists in that marvelous transfiguration of them to a condition, in respect of qualities, far above what they are, or can be in this world. Our bodies in general shall be made like the glorious body of Christ, though on earth they are but vile, "Who shall change our vile body, that it may be fashioned like unto his glorious body, according to the working, whereby he is able even to subdue all things unto himself," (Philippians 3:21).

They shall enjoy eternal health, but of the glory of the body I have entreated before, in the use of the doctrine of the resurrection. So, we see the parts of this glory. The adjuncts of it follow.

And so, there are four things in the consideration of the glory to come, which should much affect us.

1. First, that it is a glory unspeakable, that is, it is so great that no language on earth can describe it. For though we mention those foresaid parts of it, yet our narrow hearts and mouths are infinitely straitened in comparison of the full glory of man in these things, "But as it is written, The things which eye hath not seen, neither ear hath heard, neither came into man's heart, are, which God hath prepared for them, that love him," (1 Corinthians 2:9).

2. Secondly, that it is certain, and we cannot be disappointed by it. Otherwise, it would be uncomfortable to hear of so much felicity and holiness, and yet not be sure to possess it. The certainty of it, that God will bestow such glory, may appear in diverse ways.

1. There is an act or ordinance for it in God's eternal counsel. "But the foundation of God remaineth sure, and hath this seal; The Lord knoweth who are his, and, Let everyone that calleth on the name of Christ depart from iniquity," (2 Timothy 2:19). "As he hath chosen us in him, before the foundation of the world, that we should be holy, and without blame before him in love," (Ephesians 1:4). "Moreover, whom he predestinated, them also he called; and whom he called, them also he justified; and whom he justified, them he also glorified," (Romans 8:30). "Come ye blessed of my Father, inherit ye the kingdom prepared for you, from the foundations of the world," (Matthew 25:34).

2. Christ purchased it with his blood, (Ephesians 1:14).

3. Christ has made intercession when he was on earth to his Father, that he might have his redeemed ones to be where

he is, "And now am I no more in the world, but these are in the world, and I come to thee, holy Father, keep them in thy name," (John 17:11). "Father, I will that they which thou hast given me, be with me, even where I am; that they may behold my glory, which thou hast given me: for thou lovedst me before the foundation of the world," (John 17:24).

4. God has made us many promises, and given us not only his word, but his oath to assure it unto us, "So God willing more abundantly to shew unto the heirs of promise the stableness of his counsel, bound himself by an oath, that by two immutable things, wherein it is impossible that God should lie, we might have strong consolation, which have our refuge to hold fast the hope that is set before us," (Hebrews 6:17-18).

5. He has sealed to it, not only in the sacrament, but by his Spirit, which will be our witness, and is our earnest, "Wherein also after that ye believed, you were sealed with the Holy Spirit of promise. Which is the earnest of our inheritance, until the redemption of the possession purchased unto the praise of his glory," (Ephesians 1:13-14).

6. He has begun eternal life in us already.

7. Christ is gone into heaven of purpose to provide a place ready for us, "And though I go to prepare a place for you: I will come again, and receive you unto myself, that where I am, there may ye be also," (John 14:3). "Seeing therefore brethren, that by the blood of Jesus we may be bold to enter into the holy place, by the new and living way, which he hath prepared for us through the veil, which is his flesh," (Hebrews 10:19-20). So, we have its certainty.

3. The third thing is its eternity, all this glory would be less, if it were thought that it would ever end: but it shall never end, for,

1. Nothing of it shall be lost, or decay.

2. There shall be no death there: for death and hell are cast into the lake of fire.

3. There shall be no old age, or withering condition in men that possess it. It does not wither, "To an inheritance, immortal, and undefiled, and that fadeth not away, reserved in heaven for you," (1 Peter 1:4).

4. God being all in all, there shall be no weariness, no lack of the fulness of affections, or satiety, no loathing.

Divines are accustomed to shadow out eternity, by the similitude of a little bird drinking up a drop of water out of the sea; if every ten thousand years the bird should come and drink up but one drop, yet the sea might be dry at length: but yet this lasting of the sea, is nothing in comparison to the lasting of the glory of heaven.

4. Fourthly, and to these may be added its proximity. The day of the Lord is at hand. It would be some lessening of our happiness, if it were a long time to it.

FINIS

Other Works by Nicholas Byfield Published by Puritan Publications

Delivered from All Our Sins
What should a sinner first do in inquiring how to be rid of all his sins? Byfield (almost exhaustively) catalogs the Biblical sins which must be fully repented of during conversion before God. This is far different than the church pastor today who simply wants you to say the sinner's prayer. Byfield stands in complete opposition to this, and shows, biblically, how repentance ought to be sought, and what should be repented of. What Christian or God-fearer would not want to be rid of all their sins through Christ?

The Rules of a Holy Life
Are you living your life as a holy Christian? Did you know the Bible gives us directives and rules to follow that concern every area of the Christian walk? These are not Pharisaical rules, but rules that aid us to be more like Jesus Christ. In walking the Christian down the road of Christianity, Byfield teaches us what it means to be a Christian by summarizing the rules God has given us to live according to the Gospel. An outstanding work!

The Signs of a Wicked Man and the Signs of a Godly Man
Every Christian desires to be holy and pleasing in the sight of God, but they know this is only accomplished through the work of the Holy Spirit. Byfield shows the differences between godly men and wicked men in these two combined treatises that aid the Christian to discern the true marks of a believer in Jesus Christ.

The Promises of God
God has promises to his church to aid them by the power of the Holy Spirit to live a victorious life in Christ. Byfield explains how this is done, and his section on "objections and solutions" is worth the cost of this volume alone.

Directions for the Private Reading of the Scriptures
Do you have a plan for reading through the Scriptures effectively in one year? Nicholas Byfield does not only give you a plan, he explains the contents of the Bible in summary form book by book as you go!

The Assurance of God's Love
Most Christians struggle with assurance. Does God really love them, even after they've sinned again and again? This work by puritan Nicholas Byfield was one of his most popular in order to help Christians with being assured of God's love.

The Cure of the Fear of Death
I have never met a Christian who was not, at some time, afraid of death. Nicholas Byfield has a cure to help Christians overcome their fear of death.